Is the Pope Independent?

or

Outlines of the Roman Question

by

the Right Rev Mgr John Prior D.D.

Domestic Prelate of H.H. Pius X.

Published by *ROME*, Palazzo Taverna, Rome

1907

IMPRIMATUR

Fr. ALBERTUS LEPIDI O. P., S. P. Ap. Magister.

Roma — Tip. dell' Unione Coop. Editrice, via Federico Cesi, 45.

CHAPTER I.

The Rise of the Pope's Temporal Power.

Temporal dominion does not add to the spiritual power of
the Papacy — Temporal Power impossible in the beginning of the Church's history — Reasons — Society was organized on a heathen basis — The Church claims no
authority over infidels — The task of the Primitive Church,
to make the Christian ideal live in the hearts of the people
— The dawn of freedom in the edict of Milan A. D. 313
— The translation of the seat of Empire and its consequences — The barbarian invasions of Rome described by
Newman — The Popes the only protectors of the people
— Sovereignty thrust upon them — Historical view supported by Gibbon, Dollinger, Guizot.

Temporal sovereignty is not necessary for the
existence of the Church, nor does its absence dim-
inish by one tittle the spiritual jurisdiction of the
Vicar of Christ over the Universal Church. The
early Popes, like the rest of christians, were regarded as subjects of the Roman Empire, and they
obeyed its laws in all that was not sin.

These laws were in frequent conflict with the
law of God, a fact which the rulers of the Church

had constantly to emphasize by the shedding of their blood. Out of thirty Popes who reigned in the first period of the Church's history twenty-nine suffered the martyr's death. But as one after another laid down his life to testify to the faith that was in him, his successor took up the reins of spiritual government with the full power of Peter to feed the flock of Christ, until he in his turn was called upon to declare that it was better to obey God than man. Though their commands may have been issued from the imperial dungeons, they were as readily obeyed as the edicts of their remote successors that came from a throne surrounded by the homage of christian kings. Their plenary power over the Church of Christ was divine in its origin and could not be destroyed by any human agency, They were harassed and impeded in their work, but that work went on irresistibly through persecution after persecution, and the faithful for all time learnt the undying truth that the bark of Peter can ride unwrecked through the fiercest storms.

Even though the Divine founder of the Church had promised in explicit terms the prerogative of temporal rule to his Vicar on earth, it is impossible to suppose that such promise could have been realized under the ordinary ruling of providence in the early epoch of christianity. For the Church began its life in a heathen world. The atmosphere around the early christians was pervaded with paganism.

It was a physical impossibility to lift the world all at once out of the mire, to purge it in a brief space of time of its superstitions, of its pagan customs, of the immoral and idolatrous spirit that was ingrained in the laws, the life and the manners of the people. But until this necessary purgation had been in a great measure carried out, how could the Vicar of Christ sit upon an earthly throne and represent a system of law and order that kept the people in the bonds of sin? The Church makes no claim to authority over infidels — " Quid mihi de iis qui foris sunt judicare? " — If its spiritual power of legislation and judgment does not comprise these in its scope, how could it assume an earthly power over them in their collective capacity, as an organized society committed to the corruptions of heathenism?

The pagan world had first to be subjected to the yoke of Christ. The duty of the hour was to cleanse it of idolatry and rampant sin.

Its work was to make the christian ideal live in the hearts of the people before it could be reflected in public law and social economy.

This transformation was wrought by degrees under the providence and grace of God by the preaching of the Gospel, by the patience, constancy and prayers of the confessors in imprisonment and bonds, and by the blood of the martyrs, the fruitful seed of the Church.

When the first christian Emperor appeared on the throne of the Cæsars the christian Church had gained a sufficient foothold in his dominions to take its place among the free institutions of the State. The famous edict of Milan in 313 granted freedom of worship to christians throughout the Western Empire and restored the confiscated property of the Church. This act of toleration was later extended to the East. By subsequent legislation of Constantine ecclesiastics were freed from civil and military taxation; bishops received some share of judicial authority and the power to enfranchise slaves.

When the Church was thus freed from the shackles of persecution a momentous event occurred which gave its Chief Pastor in Rome ampler scope for the discharge of his high office, and opened the way to his complete independence of the civil power. This was the translation by Constantine of the seat of empire from Rome to Byzantium in the year 330. Delegates and Dukes continued to reside in Rome to rule in the name of the Emperor, but their power gradually dwindled until it became a mere shadow. Byzantium was far-distant, and as time went on the Emperors took less and less interest in their Italian

possessions. In the stress of famine and the perils
of invasion it was the Pope who came to the relief
of the people whom their nominal rulers left without protection. The exalted position of the Supreme
Pastor and his fatherly care for his flock marked
him out as their natural guardian in the troublous
times that came upon them. The treasures of the
Church were freely used to provide for the people
in the hour of need. When the hordes of barbar-
ians swept down the Italian peninsula it was the
Pope who stood between them and the inhabitants
of Rome. The terrors of these invasions have been
graphically described by Cardinal Newman in his
" Historical Essays ". " All the fury of the elements " " he writes, " was directed against it (Rome);
and, as a continual dropping wears away the stone,
so blow after blow, and revolution after revolution,
sufficed at last to heave up, and hurl down, and
smash into fragments, the noblest earthly power
that ever was. First came the Goth, then the Hun,
and then the Lombard. The Goth took possession,
but he was of noble nature, and he soon lost his
barbarism. The Hun came next; he was irreclaim-
able, but did not stay. The Lombard kept both
his savageness and his ground; he appropriated to
himself the territory not the civilisation of Italy,
fierce as the Hun, and powerful as the Goth, the
most tremendous scourge of heaven. In his dark

presence the poor remains of Greek and Roman splendour died away, and the world went more rapidly to ruin, material and moral, than it was advancing from triumph to triumph in the time of Tertullian. Alas! the change between Rome in the heyday of her pride, and in the agony of her judgment! Tertullian writes while she is exalted; Pope Gregory when she is in humiliation. He was delivering homilies on the prophet Ezekiel when the news came to Rome of the advance of the Lombards upon the city, and in the course of them he several times burst out into lamentations at the news of miseries, which eventually obliged him to cut short his exposition.

" 'Sights and sounds of war' he says 'meet us on every side. The cities are destroyed; the military stations broken up; the land devastated; the country depopulated. No one remains in the country; scarcely any inhabitant in the towns; yet even the poor remains of human kind are smitten daily and without intermission. Before our eyes some are carried away captive, some mutilated, some murdered. She herself, who once was mistress of the world, we behold how Rome fares; worn down by manifold and incalculable distresses, the bereavement of citizens, the attack of foes, the reiteration of overthrows, where is her senate? Where are her people? We, the few survivors, are still the daily prey of the sword and of other innumerable tribulations. Where are they who in a former day revelled in her glory? Where is their pomp, their pride, their frequent and immoderate joy? – young-sters, young men of the world congregated here from every quarter, where they aimed at secular advancement. Now no one hastens up to her for preferment; and so it is with other cities also; some places are laid waste by pestilence, others are de-populated by the sword, others are tormented by famine, and others are swallowed by earthquakes.' "

The Heruli, the Goths, the Visigoths, the Huns and the Lombards threatened Rome again and again with sack and ruin, and the armies of the Emperor were not there to oppose them. It was the Pope who saved Rome in the hour of her peril, not Constantinople. When Attila, "the scourge of God", advanced against Rome it was Leo the Great who went out to meet him and compelled him to retreat by the power of his apostolic word. The same Pontiff prevailed upon Genseric to withdraw from the Holy City when it was already within his power. Pope Zachary in the eighth century on two occasions saved Rome from the attacks of the Lombards.

A survey of the period from the peace of Con-stantine to the crowning of Charlemagne shows that the Popes were gradually liberated from all subjection to any civil authority; that by the force of circumstances they were compelled to discharge the office of temporal rulers in the exercise of their apostolic mission of charity to the members of their flock; that civil authority was thrust upon them by a grateful people whom for centuries they had protected when there was no one else with sufficient influence or sufficient interest to care for them; and that when at length they bore the title of temporal Sovereigns of Rome and the adjacent States — the Patrimony of St. Peter — it was but the outward expression and recognition of a power that had long been theirs.

This historical view is supported by the unimpeachable evidence of those who are above all suspicion of bias in favour of the Holy See. Let me quote but a few: Gibbon in his " Decline and Fall of the Roman Empire ", says, speaking of Rome in the 8th century: " The want of laws could only be supplied by the influence of religion, and their foreign and domestic counsels were moderated by the authority of the bishop. His alms, his sermons, his correspondence with the kings and prelates of the west, his recent services, their gratitude and oath, accustomed the Romans to consider him as the first magistrate or Prince of the city. The christian humility of the Pope was not offended by the name of Dominus or Lord; and their face and inscription are still apparent on the most ancient coins. Their temporal dominion is now confirmed by the reverence of a thousand years, and their noblest title is the free choice of a people whom they had redeemed from slavery ". — (Vol. VI, pp. 151, 152. Murray 1862).

" By the perfect inability of the Byzantine Emperors to guard the Romans, and to protect them against the attacks of the Lombards, they had forfeited their claims to those provinces; and over Rome and the Roman Dukedom, the sovereignty of the Pope had been established during the course of the 8th century... The imperial supremacy of Charlemagne was naturally extended over the States of the Church, but without any trespass on the authority of the Pontiff. The Pope continued to be what he had been, Lord of Rome, and of the Dukedom, &c.... The Pope was not, therefore, subject to the Emperor; the Romans, indeed, swore to him an oath of fidelity, but they pledged themselves with an express reservation of the fidelity due by them to the Roman Pontiff, their Sovereign ". — Dollinger, " History of the Church ", vol. III, pp. 118, 119; see Appendix, III.

Guizot, in his " L'Église et la Société " says: " The union of the spiritual and temporal power in the papacy did not arise from the systematic development either of an abstract principle, or of ambitious aims. Theories and ambitions may have been mixed with it, but that which, in spite of all obstacles, has really and truly produced the civil power of the Popes, is necessity;... an intrinsic, unceasing necessity... These earthly possessions and temporal sovereignty came to the papacy as a necessary support of his grand spiritual position... The donations of Pepin and Charles were nothing but the coping stones in the structure which began long before, and was supported by the good sense of the people and the favour of kings... As a temporal Lord the Pope roused apprehension in no one. But in his temporal sovereignty he possessed an effectual guarantee for his liberty and his moral power " (pp. 72, 142).

Chapter II.

The Necessity of Papal Independence.

The Temporal Sovereignty of the Pope a gift of Divine Providence — The battlefields of the Early Church — The Church indestructible — Normal condition in the struggles of peace — Independent of Civil Power — Allocution of Pius IX April 20 1849 — The international position of the *Servos Servorum Dei* — Attitude of the Church in temporal matters — Sovereignty of the Pope necessary in a Christian world for the *well-beiug* of the Church — Protestant testimonies: Gregorovius — British Parliament in 1849 — Lord Ellenborough — Lord Landsdowne — Lord Brougham — Lord Palmerston.

The acquisition of temporal sovereignty by the Popes was not the achievement of ambitious striving, but the natural outcome of the historical changes wrought in a world that was gradually being raised to the christian ideal. It came unsought for as the result of the christian transformation in which as heads of the Church they took a leading part. It was never regarded as the goal of their aspirations in itself, for the power confided to them by Christ was not of this world. Nor was it ever claimed

by them as an indispensable condition of the exercise
of their spiritual authority. Like Peter and his immediate successors, the later Popes could rule the
Church in a state of war as in a state of peace.
The Church, indeed, cherishes the glorious memory
of the first period of her history, and recounts day
by day in her liturgy the heroic deeds of her children
that have made its annals memorable. The faithful
seek inspiration in the courage of its martyrs, the
faith of its confessors, and the fidelity of its virgins,
so many of whom sealed their vows by the sacrifice
of their lives. What nation does not remember
with pride the battlefields where its liberties were
won? They do not, for all that, regard the state
of war as the normal condition of their existence.
Struggles follow — the struggles of peace — when
the bloody strife is over, but warfare can only be
from the nature of things a passing phase in any
organized society. Though thrones may be overturned in the shock of battles, and dynasties swept
away in the tempest of war, no such disaster can
befall the Church. No plan of attack that man or
devil could devise can destroy this work of God
or its divine constitution. However numerous, however powerful her adversaries, however fierce their
onslaught, the Church steps on to the battlefield
certain of victory. Individuals, multitudes, whole
nations may fall away from her; it is their loss,

not always hers. Were she driven back again into
the catacombs, she would emerge once more from
the darkness to reap the ripe fruit of her patient
suffering. No catholic ever fears for the fate of the
Church, whatever tears he may shed over those who
are hostile or false to her. Nevertheless, despite
her assurance of ultimate triumph in the conflicts
that may be forced upon her, she loves not war,
nor are her methods aggressive, for her mission is
one of peace.

In the fulfilment of this mission of peace to the
nations her divinely-appointed Head can be dependent on no one but God in the exercise of his
supreme and world-wide jurisdiction. He cannot,
therefore, be the subject of any earthly sovereign.
As Pius IX said in his Allocution of April 20, 1849:
" Peoples, kings and nations would never turn with
free confidence and devotion to the Bishop of Rome,
if they saw him the subject of a Sovereign or a
government and did not know him to be in possession of his full liberty. There would always arise
in them a strong suspicion and a continued fear
that the Pope in his acts yielded to the influence
of the Sovereign and the government in whose territory he dwelt. And under this pretext the decrees
of the Pontiff would oftentimes be disobeyed. „

Even the first subject of the realm is dependent,
and its peculiar interests must be paramount to him.

2

Nay, he is bound to render distinguished service
to his own country in proportion to his exalted
position. He must devote his talents, time and
labours to her welfare when they are needed. According to his power he should further her legitimate interests even when they clash with those of
other nations. One country or empire is his own,
others are foreign to him. No country is foreign
to the Pope, or all are equally so. From the
moment he ascends the throne of Peter, he ceases
to belong to any one nation; he is the common
possession of the 250 millions of his subjects scat-
tered among the kingdoms of the earth, *Servus
servorum Dei*. His position is international, or
rather supernational.

With the worldly interests of civil states he has
no direct concern. His message to his people with
regard to them is " Reddite Caesari quae sunt Cae-
saris „ — " Give to Caesar the things that are Caesar's. „ " Be loyal to your country in peace and in
war. Rest assured that in obeying lawfully-consti-
tuted authority you are obedient to the ordinance
of God. „ He confirms them in their loyalty and
patriotism. With regard to the opposing interests
of secular powers in matters that belong to their
domain his attitude is one of benevolent neutrality.
He may lend a helping hand where he will, but
without detriment or prejudice to any rival. It is

the interest of every government with catholic subjects, indeed of every government in the world,
that this neutrality should be preserved. If the
tremendous moral power which he wields over the
millions of his subjects, as the interpreter of the moral
law, the guide of their consciences and the guardian
of their religious beliefs, were made subservient to
the aims of one secular power, it would be a grievous injustice to the rest. Not only catholics, therefore, who owe the Supreme Pontiff spiritual allegiance, but secular governments are concerned in
his freedom from all subjection to civil authority.

If he cannot be the subject of any earthly power,
then he must be a sovereign; for there is no inter-
mediate state. The status of real sovereignty has
proved in the course of history the safeguard of
the independence of the Popes in the discharge of
their mission to mankind. When it came to them
as a gift of divine providence, they clung to it as
the guarantee of their freedom in their spiritual
rule, and their claim was freely acknowledged not
only by the members of the Church, but also by
protestant powers and by men who were in many
ways hostile to catholicism. Though the prerogative of temporal sovereignty was not necessary for
the being of the Church, it was necessary for its
well-being. It was not indispensable for the exercise of the Pope's supreme power over the Church

in all lands, but it was indispensable for its peaceful and independent exercise.

Let us hear the opinion and testimony, of those who can have no interest in exalting the Papacy.

Gregorovius in his *History of Rome,* vol. III, p. 5: " The Metropolis of christianity, representing a universal principle, was bound to have liberty; and full access to it was the right of the Popes; the Chief Priest who resided there could not be the subject of any king. It was this idea that preserved to the Pontiff even to our own days the small States of the Church. „ Again — " The existence of an ecclesiastical Roman State was an essential condition of the spiritual independence of the Pope „ (Italian Edit., vol. IV, p. 386).

England joined with other European powers in 1812 and 1815 in restoring Pius VII to his independence, not only as an act of justice, but as a condition of international peace.

Lord Ellenborough, on June 12th, 1849, said in the House of Lords: « It was quite true that England was not a catholic State, and might not, therefore, feel that personal interest in the position of the Pope which was felt by Catholic Powers : but we had eight millions of Roman catholic subjects, and it was as much an object of interest to us, as it would be to any one of the catholic Powers of Europe, that the Pope should be in a position of independence; that he should not be so situated as to be dependent on the bounty, or upon the power of any one, or of any combination of the Powers of Europe.

That was surely of as deep an interest to us as it would be to either Austria or Naples. The question was, not whether the Pope, as Sovereign of Rome, should or should not reside or rule there : but whether the person who happened to be the head of the Roman Catholic Religion should maintain a position of independence ; and that appeared to him to be a matter of the deepest importance ».

Lord Landsdowne said : « He did not say that they had no interest of a political character; on the contrary, he said that in his (the Pope's) political character they had the greatest interest. In that view he would repeat what he had said before, that the Government were most anxious that the Pope should be restored to Rome. He had before said, the British Government felt that it was placed in a situation quite distinct from that of the other Powers as to the restoration of the Pope. He alluded of course to the religious ties which bound those Powers to the Sovereign Pontiff, and which did not bind us. But, nevertheless, the British Government had not seen with indifference the events which had expelled the Pope from his temporal dominions: but they had always been, and still were, ready to offer such suggestions as might be useful for the purpose of restoring by negotiation the power and authority of the Pope in Rome. » (Hansard, vol. CVI, pag. 9)

Lord Brougham, on July 20th, 1849, said: " And here let me say a word which may not be popular in some quarters... upon the separation of the temporal and spiritual authority of the Pope. My opinion is that it will not do to say the Pope is all very well, as a spiritual prince, but we ought not to restore his temporal power. That is a short-sighted, and, I think, a somewhat superficial view of the case. I do not believe it possible that the Pope could exercise beneficially his spiritual functions if he had no temporal power. For what would be the consequence? He would be stripped of all authority. We are not now in the 8th century, when the Pope contrived to exist without much secular authority, or when, as Bishop of Rome, he exercised very extensive spiritual authority without corresponding temporal power. The progress of the one, however, went along with that of the other; and just as the Pope had extended his temporal dominions by encroachments and by gifts, like those of Pepin and Charlemagne... just in proportion as his temporal authority increased, did he attain so overwhelming an influence over the Councils of Europe. His temporal force increased his spiritual authority, because it made him more independent. Stripped of that secular dominion he would then become the slave now of one Power — then of another — one day the slave of Spain, another of Austria, and another of France, or, worst of all, as the Pope has recently been, the slave of his own subjects. His temporal power is an European question, not a local or a religious one, and the Pope's authority should be maintained for the sake of the peace and the interests of Europe. We ourselves have seven million of Roman Catholic subjects... and how is it possible to suppose that, unless the Pope has enough temporal authority to keep him independent of the other European Courts, jealousies and intrigues will not arise which must reduce him to a state of dependency?... and so enable any one country wielding the enormous influence of his spiritual authority to foster intrigues, factions, and rebellion in the dominion of her rivals." (Hansard, vol. CVII, p. 627).

Lord Landsdowne answered as follows: " He had no hesitation in stating that he quite agreed with the views of his noble and learned friend on the subject; but he assured him that they were by no means peculiar, inasmuch as they were precisely those laid down in Lord Palmerston's despatch to Lord Normanby, where he distinctly declared that the sovereignty of the Pope was something quite peculiar, and, having a relation with all the Roman Catholic States of the world, quite different from that of any other authority. The condition of the Pope's Sovereignty was quite peculiar. As a Temporal Sovereign the Pope was of a fourth or fifth rate order: as a Spiritual Sovereign he was not only of the first order, but enjoyed a Sovereignty unparalleled in the world, being capable of exercising over, not one, but every country in Europe an authority and influence with which nothing could compare. There was, therefore, in respect of other States, a ground for interfering and maintaining his authority, which did not exist in any other case; and being a sort of compound interest, the necessity was imposed on the Catholic Powers of watching, in order to see that the joint object of preserving the Head of their religion was not made the means of promoting temporal ambition. But when he said that, he was not prepared to say that we as a Protestant State, had not, to a certain extent, a similar interest: there was not a country with Catholic subjects, and Catholic possessions, which had not a deep interest in the Pope being so placed as to be able to exercise his authority unfettered and unshackled by any temporal influence which might affect his spiritual authority." (Hansard, vol. CVII, p. 707).

Lord Palmerston's despatch to Lord Normanby was, in substance, as follows: " That it is without doubt to be desired that a person, who in his spiritual character exercises vast influence in the internal affairs of the greater part of the nations of Europe should be so independent as not to become, in the hands of any European power whatsoever, a means of embarrassing others."

———

Chapter III.

International Character of the Roman Question.

Declaration of the Spanish Prime Minister in 1885 — Author-
itative statements and official reports of Italian Ministers
Cavour — Visconti-Venosta, Italian Minister of Foreign
Affairs — Italian Minister at Berne — Minghetti, Italian
Minister at Vienna — Carlo Cadorna, Italian Minister at
at London — Italian Minister at Brussels — Italian Mi-
nister at Madrid — The Decree of October 9, 1870 —
Solemn pledge of Victor Emmanuel II — The day after
the seizure of Rome — The disappearance of the Temporal
Power — Chief provisions of the Law of Guarantees.

The foregoing quotations from English statesmen,
together with the testimonies of different protestant
writers, may be read in Cardinal Manning's little
book entitled " The Independence of the Holy See."
Evidence of the same kind, showing the general recognition, even in protestant States, of the great
principle underlying the fact of the temporal sov-
reignty of the Papacy, it would be easy to multiply.
A Roman Professor, many years ago, went to the
trouble of collecting passages from the political
speeches of men in public life, from State docu-

ments and from the writings of well-known men in
different countries illustrating this principle into a
book, which he called " Fiore di Sentenze politiche,
o Detti Memorabili intorno il Papato e l'Italia, scelti
da statisti d'ogni nazione ed ordinati in tre libri dal
prof. D. F." For the purpose of this brief essay,
in which I am endeavouring to give the outlines
of the Roman question from the copious literature
on the subject, I need only add to the protestant
testimonies already quoted the views expressed by
the government of Catholic Spain, before I proceed
to lay before my readers the important declarations
of the Italian government both before and after the
occupation of Rome. Canovas del Castillo, the
Spanish Prime Minister, speaking in the Chamber
of Deputies on Jan. 19, 1885, said: — " This independence of the Pontifical Power is not a thesis
belonging exclusively to the Holy See, even though
the Holy See may give it, exercising its own right,
a definite form; it is not a thesis belonging exclusively to the Spanish government, nor to any other
foreign government: it is the thesis of the Italian
government itself, which has, therefore, rightly established the Law of Guarantees. For the affirmation
of the principle of the independence of the Papacy
is the affirmation of a common principle. How will
effect be given to such independence? How is effect
being given to it? This is a question on which

others may be more or less in agreement; which
may be solved in one way or another in the future:
but this is not the question at present before the
Spanish government. As a question of principle,
yes; the Spanish government maintains, as the Italian government, the absolute necessity of the independence of the Pontifical Power." Again, on
Feb. 6, 1885, he said: — " There is no one to-day
in Europe who believes that the independence of
the Pope is a purely Italian interest, and does not
belong to the whole catholic world. No; this opinion is not the profession of Europe; nor is it the
profession of the Italian government, to judge by
the Law of Guarantees and much less does it appear to be so, if we recall the explanations given
by its ministers when they were under discussion.
This is an opinion which nobody sustains... No;
the question of the independence of the Papacy,
under whatever form it may present itself in history,
or in whatever manner it may come before us to-day
will always be a question that regards the entire
catholic world. What I think, many catholics think,
the immense majority, not to say the entire body
of catholics, and it is that a certain historical form
of the independence of the Papacy is most fitting,
is of the highest importance, not absolutely or as
a matter of rigorous dogma, and is necessary to
this same independence." The value of this guarded

statement by the Prime Minister of Spain is en-
hanced by the fact that it was delivered fifteen
years after the seizure of Rome, during which time
friendly diplomatic relations subsisted between Spain
and Italy.

The declarations of the Italian government, both
before and after the occupation of Rome, in State
documents, diplomatic circulars and ministerial utterances in parliament acknowledge the same principle, namely, that the Head of the Universal Church
must be independent of civil authority, and the security of his independence is a matter which affects
not only Italy, but also the catholic world in general
and all governments with catholic subjects. Father
G. Zocchi S. J. has collected a series of these authoritative pronouncements in his book " Papa e Re "
(page 247 and seq.) from which I take most of the
following.

Cavour said in a speech delivered in the Chamber
on March 24, 1861; — " We must go to Rome,
but on two conditions: we must go there in agreement with France; and in such a way that the
uniting of this City with the kingdom of Italy may
not be interpreted by the great mass of catholics
in Italy and outside Italy as a sign of the enslaving
of the Church. We must go to Rome, but without
bringing about any diminution of the independence
of the Pope. We must go to Rome, but without

allowing the civil authority to extend its power to
the spiritual order. If we succeed in realizing the
the second of the above-mentioned conditions, the
first will not present many difficulties; if we succeed in uniting Rome to Italy without arousing
grave fears in the catholic body; if we, I say, succeed in persuading the great mass of catholics that
the union of Rome with Italy can be made without
the Church ceasing to be independent, I think the
problem will be solved. "

In the " Gazzetta Ufficiale " of Sept. 11, 1870,
there appeared a circular sent by Visconti-Venosta,
Minister of Foreign Affairs, to His Majesty's Ministers abroad. The circular bore the date of Florence,
29 August, 1870, and said that Italy " is called upon
to regulate with the catholic world the conditions
of the transformation of the Pontifical Power," and
the Minister appealed for " the moral adhesion of
catholic governments. " The answer of Austria was
that they were deeply interested in the Roman
Question, and they counted on the intention of the
Italian government, manifested on several occasions,
not by itself to solve the question, and recommended
Italy not to increase the trepidation of the catholic
world.

The Italian Minister at Berne in a despatch of
September 6, 1870, wrote to Visconti-Venosta. " It
must not be thought that the (Swiss) Confederation

is indifferent to the religious interests of its catholic population; rather will it safeguard them in every event. The Executive Federal Power, therefore, takes cognisance of the promise made by the King's government of its intention to come to an understanding with the Powers in order to secure the essential conditions of the liberty and spiritual independence of the Holy See, conditions, in whose maintenance on the part of the Italian government the liberty of conscience guaranteed by the Federal Constitution to all the Swiss is greatly interested, and without which, in any case, the catholic nations would refuse their consent to our sovereignty over Rome becoming an accomplished fact. "

Marco Minghetti, Italian Minister at Vienna, wrote on September 10, 1870: " All, catholics and non-catholics, are preoccupied concerning the liberty and independence of the Holy See. Hence the plan proposed by the Italian government to come to an understanding on this point with the other Powers is acknowledged as wise and opportune in order to avoid future complications. "

Carlo Cadorna, Italian Minister at London, wrote on September, 8, 1870 that he had spoken with Lord Granville and assured him that the Italian government " is resolved to give and establish for the independence and liberty of the Pope, ordained for the exercise of his spiritual power, all the guarantees which are required by the religious liberty itself of Italian citizens, and by the religious interests of the other catholic nations of Europe. "

Carlo de Barral, Italian Minister at Brussels, wrote on September 12, 1870, that he had seen Mr D'Anéthan, at that time head of the Belgian government, who expressed himself in the following terms: "Absolutely speaking, temporal power was not of indispensable necessity to the Holy See in order to accomplish its mission in the world, but, nevertheless, some compromise must be found at all costs, something which would allow the Pope to exercise his spiritual functions with full and entire freedom of action; without its being even possible to imagine that the least foreign pressure or influence entered in: this something, he added, should receive the collective guarantee of the great Catholic Powers. "

Marcello Cerruti, Italian Minister at Madrid, wrote on September 29, 1870 that General Prim declared to him: "One only thing is essential, one only thing dominates all the rest, and on this the Spanish government, proud of a title (His Catholic Majesty) appertaining to the Spanish Crown, considers it right to insist: that is, the perfect spiritual independence of the Head of the Catholic Religion, and the perfect personal liberty of the Supreme Pontiff."

3

On October 9, 1870 a decree was issued by which Rome was annexed to the Italian Kingdom; it contained these words: " The Sovereign Pontiff preserves the dignity and inviolability and all the personal prerogatives of sovereignty by a law for this purpose which will be sanctioned, and all conditions required to guarantee it, together with its territorial liberties and the free exercise of the authority of the Holy See."

On September 8, 1870, twelve days before he entered Rome by the breach of Porta Pia, King Victor Emanuel wrote in these words to Pius IX: " The government of the King will protect the interest which the whole catholic world possesses in the entire independence of the Sovereign Pontiff " (Samver, Recueil des Traités, tom. V, p. 33).

On September 21, 1870, the day after the conquest of Rome, Visconti-Venosta, Minister of Foreign Affairs, in a letter to the Italian Minister at Vienna begged friendly governments to associate themselves with Italy in a work fruitful for European civilization, taking cognisance of the guarantees which the Italians wished to offer to the Holy Father. Among these guarantees he proposed a civil list, " guaranteed, if need be, by a public treaty." And he added: " The governments having catholic subjects would fulfil a noble mission by negotiating in favour of the Head of the Church guarantees which would completely reassure their consciences."

The Italian government, then, gave their fullest acknowledgement to the principle of the independence of the Pope, admitted freely that the Roman question was not an Italian, but an international one, invited the different governments to cooperate with them in reassuring the catholic world that the independence of the Holy See would not be interfered with, and gave the most solemn pledges that they would provide for its security in an adequate and satisfactory manner.

With the entry of the Italian troops into Rome the Pope ceased to exercise the rights of sovereignty over any portion of the ancient Pontifical States. His temporal dominion, which had served for a thousand years as a safeguard of his spiritual position, came to an end. The safeguard, which the Italian government offered him as an adequate substitute of his vanished temporal power, is contained in the Law of Guarantees passed on the 13th of May 1871. Here are its chief provisions : —

Prerogatives of the Sovereign Pontiff and the Holy See

Art. 1. The person of the Sovereign Pontiff is sacred and inviolable.

Art. 2. Any attempt against the person of the Sovereign Pontiff and of provocation to commit the same shall be punished with the same penalties as any attempts against the person of the King. The offences and insults publicly committed directly against the person of the Pontiff by speeches or acts, or by the means indicated by the first article of the law concerning the press, to be punished with the same penalties fixed by the 19th article of the same law.

Art. 3. The Italian government pays to the Sovereign Pontiff within the territory of the kingdom the sovereign honours and pre-eminences accorded to him by Catholic Sovereigns.

Art. 12. The Sovereign Pontiff may correspond freely with the Episcopate and the whole of the catholic world without any interference on the part of the Italian government.

Art. 13. In the City of Rome and the six suburbicarian bishoprics, the seminaries, the academias
the schools and the other catholic institutes founded
for the education and the culture of ecclesiastics,
shall continue to depend solely on the Holy See
without any interference of the scholastic authorities of the kingdom.

———

CHAPTER IV.

The Law of Guarantees and the Powers.

How the Law fails — Diplomatic relations with Italy no sanction of the Law — A Spanish Minister explains — The Berlin Congress — Roman Question " more than international " — Powers in an attitude of reserve — Italy experiments on its own responsibility — Why the Powers do not intervene — The nations support the Papal protest — The Emperor of Austria — Protestant Sovereigns and the Vatican etiquette — The question still open.

What I have to say about this Law of Guarantees may be stated under the following heads, which I shall proceed briefly to explain:

1. It has never been sanctioned by the Powers.

2. It has not been observed by the Italian Government.

3. It contains radical and essential defects.

4. It has been persistently rejected by the Popes.

The Law of Guarantees, established by the Italian Government to settle an international question in which the interests of all civilized governments are concerned, has never received the sanction of those governments. It is true that the different nations have diplomatic relations with United Italy, and she has been admitted into the circle of the Great Powers. But such international relations do not constitute an approval of her conquest of Rome, much less a sanction of the settlement by which she pretends to provide for the independent position of the Pope. A Spanish Deputy, Emilio Castelar, who at one time inveighed against the Law of Guarantees and called Victor Emanuel " the Pope's Gaoler," became afterwards an ardent supporter of the House of Savoy, and put forward the plea in debate that the recognition accorded to United Italy by the establishment of diplomatic relations with her involved the approval of the position which she had taken up in Rome. He was answered in the following terms by the Minister, Marquis de Pidal, on the 14th of February 1885: " Such a theory I have never read in any authoritative pubblication... The recognition of a nation does not imply approval of all the acts which constitute its history, and this is so obvious that no writer has ever asserted the contrary. Nor could a writer be regarded as of any authority who did affirm it. If Mr Castelar wants an example of what I say, I will supply him with one of great weight — the action of the Church herself. Remember what happened when the American Republics threw off the rule of Spain. At that time the Church, the Holy See, recognized those Republics, and in answer to the question whether such recognition approved of the rebellion of the Republics against the Spanish Government, the Holy See said that in ecclesiastical international law a recognition by the continuance of negotiations regarding the religious and spiritual interests of catholics, whose control rested with the Church, did not imply the approval of all the political acts which accompanied the constitution of those Republics. "

I have read in a work entitled " La questione romana e l'Europa politica " by a Roman Professor (vol. I, pag. 327) that Count Corti, the Italian representative at the Berlin Congress, tried to obtain the consent of the representatives of other Powers to a diplomatic sanction of the occupation of Rome, and he was told by Waddington, Lord Beaconsfield and Count Andrassey that if the proposal was as much as submitted to the Congress, they would at once leave the assembly.

The different Governments have never surrendered the position they constantly maintained before the taking of Rome, namely, that the independence of the Pope is an international question, or in the words of Visconti-Venosta in the Italian Parliament on the 22nd of April 1871, "more than international." (Atti uff. della Camera, pag. 776).

They have not taken positive action. They have been content to look on and reserve their judgment

and their right to intervene, while Italy made its
experiment with its Law of Guarantees. As Visconti-Venosta, Italian Minister of Foreign Affairs,
said in the House on the 30th of January 1871:
" The Governments left to our responsibility and
to the responsibility of our acts, and reserved to
themselves the right to judge, the proof which we
have announced that we are able to give that, after
the cessation of the Temporal Power, the Pontiff
will continue to exercise his functions with freedom
and dignity. " (Atti uff., pag. 435). We have seen
the Concert of the Powers regulating important
matters in Turkey, Greece, Morocco and elsewhere,
but why have they never ventured to touch the
Roman Question? Is it not, on the one hand, that
they have no satisfactory solution to offer of the
situation brought about by the spoliation of the
Pope, and on the other, that they regard their own
peculiar interests as sufficiently safe as long as the
Pope persists in his attitude of protest against the
despoilers? There are, doubtless, statesmen in the
Cabinets of Europe who would like to see the
Papacy destroyed root and branch. But with the
responsibility of government on their shoulders they
must recognize it as a grand fact which confronts
the world on every side, and remains to be reckoned
with in many contingencies.

Moreover, facts are not wanting to show that the Pope has received some measure of support from the Powers in his protest against the condition to which he has been reduced by the Italian Revolution, which robbed him of his Principality. King Humbert paid an official visit to the Emperor of Austria and thereby laid upon him the obligation of making a return visit to his Court at Rome. That return visit was never paid, because the Emperor of Austria, with the advice of his Government, chose rather to commit what, under ordinary circumstances, would be considered a grave act of discourtesy against a friendly Power and an ally, than seem to sanction by his presence in Rome the dispositions of the Law of Guarantees. No Catholic Sovereign or Head of a Catholic State has visited Rome since 1870 with the one exception of the President of the French Republic a few years ago, when the French Government had already resolved to make war on the Papacy and the Church in France. Even the Protestant Sovereigns, like the Emperor of Germany and the Head of the British Empire, who have been the guests of the King of Italy, have left Italian territory as it were, by retiring to their own Embassies, before paying their visit of compliment to the Head of the Church. This etiquette is not laid down by the Law of Guarantees; it is required by the Sovereign Pontiff as one of the many ways by which he makes known to the world his protest against his condition of dependence, and as such it has been complied with by the Protestant Sovereigns in friendly visit at the Italian Court.

The attitude of the Powers, then, in spite of amicable relations and alliances with Italy, though an attitude of waiting, is not one of indifference, and shows that the Roman Question, as far as they are concerned, is still an open one, and has not found its solution in the Law of Guarantees.

CHAPTER V.

Italy violates the Law of Guarantees.

Italian Courts of Cassation explain an important provision of
the Law — " The Pope on a level with the person of the
King" — A Liberal Newspaper condemns continuous insults against the Pope — What is happening to-day in
Rome — The *Civiltà Cattolica* denounces the offending
Press — Attack on the funeral procession of Pius IX —
"Into the river with the Pope" — Leo XIII protests that
he is made a prisoner in the Vatican — Government
despatch contradicted by Roman Court of Appeal — The
commemorative medal — Why the Pope cannot leave the
Vatican — Theodoli-Martinucci case — The Pope's Mag-
giordomo cited before an Italian Court — The funds of
Propaganda seized by the Government — Pontifical Colleges
lose control of their property — Tardy restitution by the
Government.

The Law of Guarantees has not been observed
by the Italian Government. That law, according
to a sentence delivered by the Court of Cassation
of Rome on the 23rd of July 1887 "assures *the
dignity*, the independence and the decorum of the
Sovereign Pontiff." The Court of Cassation of
Naples defines " that the Law of May 13 1871 pun-
ishes public offences and insults against the person

of the Supreme Pontiff, declared sacred and inviolable, whatever the function of the Pontiff, to which
the insult has reference. " The Court of Cassation
of Turin says in still more explicit terms: — " The
Law of Guarantees, *which puts the Pope on a level
with the Person of the King*, must be interpreted
and applied as it is written, without restrictions
or conditions. Hence, after the verdict of a Jury
proclaiming the guilt of a person accused of having
offended the Supreme Pontiff by means of the Press,
there is no efficacy in the plea that the offence was
directed against not the Head of the Church but
against a pretender and a conspirator. "

How this provision of the Law has been observed
in former years, we may gather from an article in
the liberal newspaper *L'Opinione* on the 9th of
August 1881. It says: — " We have a Law of
Guarantees. Thereby is acknowledged the spiritual
sovereignty of the Pontiff, to whom must be rendered those honours that belong to a Sovereign.
Hence, an offence against the Pope is not only not
in any way permitted, but is severely punished by
the law. Now, since 1876 (*since 1870 would have
been more correct*) the Government has declined to
notice the insulting words against the Pope, published time after time in certain journals, and uttered
at certain meetings; but the public that does not
know nor understand subtle distinctions, has been

authorized to believe that in this respect the Law of Guarantees has ceased to have any value.

" In the meeting at the Politeama, some speakers spoke of the Pope as the worst of rogues, yet no guardian of the public peace ventured to impose silence. The Ministry and the Police only then began to move when the promotors of the meeting brought forward a resolution calling on the people to take possession of the Pontifical Palaces. But if, yielding to the entreaties of the police, who acted on behalf of the Ministry, the leaders had consented to modify that resolution, the Government would probably have announced through its official organs that the proceedings had been conducted with order and in perfect accordance with the law. "

There has been no change in the policy of the Government since 1881 to our own day, as we who have lived in Rome have reason to remember. An article in the *Civiltà Cattolica* of the Ist of March of this year 1907 shows how things stand at present. It says : — "Unfortunately this is the fact, as shameful as it is painful, which we denounce today before the whole world, before all honest men, Italians and strangers. For some time past the antireligious and immoral press of Rome and Italy, and notably an unclean weekly sheet, the most lurid of the representatives of pornography and impiety, does nothing but commit outrage, fouling all that is pure and sacred and aiming principally at the sacred person of the Pontiff, exciting against him the hatred and contempt of the populace, by calumnies, buffoonery, insult and shameless and obscene caricatures.

" This fact is public and notorious. It goes on continuously under the eyes of all Romans, nay of all Italians and of the numbers of strangers that visit our cities. It is repeated every day under the very windows, so to speak, and at the very doors of the Minister of Grace and Justice, of the Police Authorities, of the Executive, of the Royal Procurator.

" But the Minister of Grace and Justice and the Police have no eyes for the fact; the Executive is deaf to it; the Royal Procurator is mute. A law, defined by the Council of State as " among the most important and fundamental of the State " is publicly and repeatedly trodden under foot, and the authorities allow this to go on! Not only do they not act officially as they ought to do, and as certainly and laudably they would act if the caricatures, buffoonery, and insults were directed against the person of the King; but, worse still, they pay no real attention to the denunciations made to them in all legal ways by distinguished citizens, utterly disgusted not only by the connivance of the authorities and the brutal vulgarity of the offences but by the shameful spectacle of the brazen impudence with which the law is openly violated by men who publicly boast of their impunity.

" How can it be said that the sovereignty of the Pontiff is guaranteed by the third article of the law, when neither his dignity, nor his name, nor his personal character is guaranteed? Are sovereign honours rendered by those who allow him to be insulted with impunity in the sight of all Rome and of all Italy? "

If the Sovereign Pontiff has not suffered personal injury, it is due to the protecting walls of the Vatican rather than to the vigilance and solicitude of the Italian Government. On the 13th of July 1881 the body of Pius IX was translated from St. Peter's to its final resting-place in the crypt of San Lorenzo outside the Walls. Notice of the translation had been given to the Government. When the small funeral cortège reached the Bridge of St. Angelo it was broken into by a band of ruffians with cries of — " A fiume il Papa ! — A fiume ! Morte al Papa, morte ai Preti ! " — " Into the river with the Pope ! — Into the river ! Death to the Pope, death to the Priests ! " Had not stout opposition been offered by the faithful who walked in the procession, the assailants might have carried out their sacrilegious intent, and the body of the deceased Pontiff been thrown into the Tiber. The

4

inference from this fact was obvious. If the sacred
remains of the dead Pope were not free from violation when they were borne to the grave, what
would happen to a living Pope who presented
himself in the streets of Rome? Leo XIII, speaking
of this outrage in his allocution on the 4th of August 1881, said: — "It is clearer than ever that
we cannot remain in Rome otherwise than as pri-
soners in the Vatican." And the Cardinal Secretary of State wrote to the Papal Nuncios — "The
imprisonment of the Pontiff has been proved by a
lamentable but incontrovertible fact. And now
every one can see what is the practical worth of
the much-lauded Guarantees, which reduce the Pope
in reality to a lower condition than that of the
last Bishop in Italy, who is, at least, free to go to
his Cathedral to celebrate there the sacred rites,
and after death may be carried with marks of respect in peace to the grave."

Mancini, the Italian Secretary for Foreign Affairs, telegraphed his view of the incident to the
different Governments on the 27th of July, attri-
buting the disorders to provocation and seditious
cries on the part of the catholics who accompanied
the procession. This lying statement could hardly
have reached its destination when on this same
day of the 27th of July, the following sentence was
solemnly delivered in the Court of Appeal in

Rome : — " In vain has the plea of provocation
been put forward ; for the beginning of the disorders was due to persons extraneous to the function ; and nothing was done by those who formed
the cortege which was out of keeping with the
regulations of a pious ceremony. " Only a small
penalty, however, with no proportion to the gra-
vity of the offence, was inflicted. The convicted
persons were heroes in the eyes of their party, and
a medal was coined in honour of the blow they
had struck against the Papacy. It bore on one side
the legend " Immortale odium et nunquam sanabile
vulnus, " with the name of a ringleader " Pio
Scatizzi ; " on the other side were the words —
" Ai Romani — che giudicarono — il Papato
— la sera — del 13 Luglio 1881. " — " To the
Romans who judged the Papacy on the evening
of July 13 1881. "

The Minister of Foreign Affairs took this opportunity of announcing, by way of making his
explanations to foreign Governments more complete,
that the Pope was free to go through the streets
of Rome if he was not applauded by the faithful,
adding that his egress from the Vatican would be
a manifest proof that he recognized the Kingdom
of Italy with Rome as its Capital. If any one seeks
for a reason why the Pope remains constantly
shut up within the Vatican Palace, he will find it

in this ministerial despatch, and in the lesson conveyed by the event I have just narrated.

The Italian soldiers have not yet ventured to cross the threshold of the Vatican, but the action of the Roman Court of Appeal, backed by the Government of the day in the Theodoli - Martinucci case, calls upon the people to believe that the writ of Italy's King runs in the Papal Palace as it does beyond its precincts. Monsignor Theodoli, the Pope's Maggiordomo, dismissed from the Pope's service in the year 1882 the Chief of the Vatican Fire-Brigade. Feeling himself aggrieved, this official, instead of appealing to the regular tribunals in the Vatican, brought an action for wrongful dismissal against the Papal Maggiordomo in the Italian Courts. The Maggiordomo refused to recognize their jurisdiction, but they formally declared themselves competent, judged the case, and decided against the plaintiff. He carried the matter to the Court of Appeal, and this Court decided as the lower Court had done, that it was competent to deal with the case, and confirmed the verdict previously given. The actual subject of litigation was in the last degree insignificant. But the principle at stake was of the highest importance, and it was commonly understood that the Court would not have ventured to deal with a matter regarding the Pope's household without previons consultation with the Government. And what becomes of the sovereignty and independence of the Pope, if he cannot discharge a servant without being liable to be called to account for it before an Italian Tribunal? As Windthorst said in his speech on this matter at the German Catholic Congress on the 14th of September 1882 — "Such is the extra-territoriality and immunity referred to by the (Italian) Minister of Foreign Affairs! The Pope must put his servants under the jurisdiction of Italian justice, that is, the Pope must be a subject of the Kingdom of Italy."

It is owing to the wise discretion of the Popes, and to the peaceful character of their protest that such conflicts have not been more frequent. While they have never abated their claims against the unjust spoliation, in the practical assertion of those claims they have sought to avoid any action that might lead to the embitterment of the struggle, or afford a pretext for futile encounters.

The propagation of the faith among the Heathen has always been one of the chief duties of the Head of the Universal Church, and nearly 300 years ago the Popes instituted in Rome a special department of administration to promote, and regulate, and assist this work. It was provided with the necessary material funds, which in the course of time accumulated to a goodly sum,

bearing some proportion to the vast cosmopol-
itan and civilizing work for which it was needed.
In the year 1884 the Italian Government swept
these funds into its own treasury. It pays an annual interest, but the capital is sunk irredeemably
in what is called Italian *vinculated consols*. No
part of it can be realized at any time to meet a
passing emergency, as was often found necessary
in the past. The late conversion of the Italian
Debt from 4 per cent to 3 $^1/_2$, and by automatic
process in five year's time to 3 per cent, diminshes
the interest paid without giving the option of a
sale. This is legalized robbery. The same pre-
datory hand was laid on the property of the Pontifical Colleges, institutions provided by the Popes
to help in mission work throughout the Church.
In them priests are trained under the direction of
the Holy Father, independently of the hierarchies
of the different countries to which they are sent.
It is his special contribution, as the Common Father of the faithful, to the labours of the worldwide
Church in various parts of the globe. The English
College is one of them, and its Directors, like those
of other similar institutions, had to look on helplessly
while their property was sold by auction and the
proceeds seized by the Government.

Other religious bodies, gathered in the Mother-
Houses of their Orders in Rome, and specially needed

by the Holy Father in his central administration of the Church, fared still worse, for their property was confiscated, and no sort of compensation was given, although a clause in the Law of Guarantees pledged the Government to leave them untouched. For such property seized in the year 1873 the Italian Govenment made partial restitution the other day by paying over to the Cardinal Vicar of Rome the sum of 360,000 pounds sterling, thereby acknowledging the unlawful spoliation.

If I were giving an account of the persecution of the Church by the Italian Government, I should have to speak of a great many other things ; of their refusal to allow lawfully-appointed Bishops to take possession of the temporalities of their Sees ; of the wholesale suppression of Convents and Religious Houses, and the turning adrift upon the world of so many of their inmates ; of the imposition of military service on clerics ; of the immunity accorded in so many ways to the most violent enemies of the Church. Fortunately a better spirit prevails in the counsels of the Italian Ministry at the present moment, for which we must give them credit. But this general question is beyond my present purpose, which is merely to point out some grave instances in which they have violated their own law.

Chapter VI.

The unique character of the Papal Temporal Power.

The test of the Law of Guarantees — The Church an organized Society with a spiritual end — Its interests higher
than those of the State — The action of the Bishops and
clergy of France — The Church a Perfect Society and
perpetual — The right of conquest and the accomplished
fact — The unique position of the Pope — Prescription
impossible — Italian revolutionaries face to face with the
world-wide Church — The Catholic demand — The means
of its enforcement — The makers of United Italy acknowledge the justice of this demand — Minghetti, Visconti-
Venosta, Senator Mameli.

The Law of Guarantees contains radical and essential defects.

The Law must be judged in relation to the end
for which it was made, namely, to ensure the freedom
and independence of the Pope in the discharge of
his high office, as Head of the Universal Church.
Our estimate of its sufficiency or insufficiency must
be based on its adequacy or inadequacy to accomplish
this purpose. At the risk of repetition, I will state
a few facts and principles that may throw into relief the situation, brought about by the successful

invasion of the Papal States and the occupation of
Rome, which called forth the Law of Guarantees.

The Universal Church comprises its 250 millions of
subjects, in every land and clime, gathered together
in the bonds of unity by the marvellous organization of its Hierarchy, under its Chief Pastor, who
wields authority over all the faithful in their individual and collective capacity. The end of the
Church, to which all its activity is directed, is the
spiritual well-being of its subjects; and those subjects hold as a cardinal principle, rooted in natural
and divine law, that mere temporal well-being must
give way where it is an obstacle to the spiritual
interests of the soul. Should the commands of the
State, with its charge of the temporal interests of
its citizens, come into collision with those of the
Church in its legitimate sphere, the latter must prevail. In other words, God must be obeyed rather
than man. The Bishops and clergy in France, the
other day, contrary to the will and intention of the
Government, refused obedience to the law of the
land, and elected to bear the penalty in the immediate loss of property to the extent of sixteen million pounds with all the hardships which that loss
entailed, and the prospect of further persecution,
rather than prove unfaithful to the Church. But
the action of the Church in normal conditions confirms the authority of the State. There are no

truer patriots, more upright citizens, nor more loyal
and devoted subjects than Catholics who live up to
the teachings of their Church. The Church is a
Perfect Society, with all the means at its command
for the attainment of its own end. It exists be-
side the State, but independently of it, both in its
origin and its permanence, and it will remain for all
time. States may attack it; they may cripple it
for a time; they cannot annihilate it. Even unbelievers, who know not the divine promises, which
are the sufficient pledge of its perpetuity to Catholics, have learnt the lesson of its two thousand
years of history, and know that it will not die. It
is this world-wide Society that claims the freedom
and independence of its Head.

When the Italian revolution overturned one
throne after another in its career of conquest, it
assumed the sovereign rule of the exiled Princes
in Parma, and Modena, and Tuscany, and Naples.
It was the Government *de facto*, and the people
obeyed it as such, many of them preserving in their
heart their allegiance to their former rulers. When
the lapse of time showed the impossibility of restoring the fallen dynasties, then the Government *de
facto* became also the Government *de jure*, for the
right of the people to orderly and peaceful government must prevail over the right of the individual
Prince to be invested with the sovereign power.

The right of conquest was confirmed, — the revolution became an accomplished fact. When the Pontifical States, however, were seized, there was question not merely of the disappearance of a temporal dynasty, venerable beyond all others as the oldest in Europe and the best founded in right, but of something far more momentous. The temporal power, on which violent hands had been laid, had been vested in one who was at the same time the Supreme Spiritual Ruler of the mightiest organization that the world had known. History could show many examples of supreme religious and secular power united in the same person, but the secular power had been the principal prerogative, the religious the accessory. Here it was the reverse. The temporal power of the Roman Pontiff was of small moment in itself, but derived immense importance from its relation to the Spiritual Power, of which it was the shield. The position of the Sovereign Pontiff was unique, and without a parallel in history. Could prescription ever corroborate conquest here, when the mighty Spiritual Power must endure undiminished, with its need for protection? Could the lapse of time ever sanction the act of violence by which the secular ward of the great Spiritual Power had been wrested away?

The irruption of the armed forces of Italy into Rome, the last stronghold of the Papal States,

brought the Italian revolutionaries face to face with
the world-wide Church, which demanded and insisted
on the freedom and independence of its Head, —
freedom and independence, which for over a thousand years had been, and in the opinion of the catholic and protestant world up to that time, could
only be, safeguarded by the possession of territory,
where he was Temporal Lord and Master. Italy
had destroyed this bulwark of his independence;
what could they offer as an adequate substitute?
The catholic demand was unmistakeably clear. Their
Head must be independent; he must be free from
any extraneous influence in the use of the tremendous moral power to which they owed obedience;
he must be untrammelled in his relations with Temporal Rulers, and accessible to all his subjects at
all times; he held a throne of which no human
power could deprive him, and he must be surrounded
with the reverence and decorum befitting his exalted
dignity.

Italy's military achievements were at an end;
she was now confronted with a moral power of
immeasurable dimensions which her weapons could
not reach. Catholics in all lands could bring the
weight of public opinion to bear upon the usurpers
of the Papal dominions; they could put pressure
upon their own Governments, which, even without
that pressure, had their own interest in seeing that

the great moral power of the Papacy should not be placed at the service of the New Italy. Such potent and combined influences might at some unforeseen moment set armies in motion to drive the temporary victors from the sacred domain where they had dared to pitch their tents. It was not a spirit of generosity to a conquered foe, nor respect for the sacred office of the Vicar of Christ, but the inexorable necessity of the case, that moved the responsible rulers of Italy to give some sort of satisfaction to the catholic demands.

The makers of United Italy frankly recognized the imperious force of facts, and, before the invasion of Rome, gave solemn pledges, to which I have already referred, to the European Governments that the freedom and independence of the Pope should remain unchanged. I may here be allowed to add one or two more explicit utterances on the point by Italy's responsible Statesmen. Minghetti said in the Italian Parliament on the 24th of January 1871. — "Since the Pope has relations with the whole world, since he is, and wishes to be considered, a Sovereign not only by Italian catholics, but also by catholics spread in every nation, we, gentlemen, cannot prescind from this situation, and we must place the Pope in such an eminent position that the idea that he may be a subject of the King of Italy cannot enter the mind of any one." The Minister

of Foreign Affairs, Visconti-Venosta, in the parliamentary sitting of the 20th of January 1871, used
the following words: — "Gentlemen, by the common
law alone, we can create no other position for the
Pope than that of an Italian subject. He who is
not a subject, is a Sovereign. This condition of
the Pope exists by the force of things, through the
actual organization of Catholicism, which we are
unable to alter, and, whether there be a sanction
or not, the Governments that have catholic subjects
will always consider that in this situation there is
for everybody an international interest." The Senator Mameli, in the sitting of April the 21st, 1871,
said: — "The Pope holds the rights of a Sovereign,
not by the grace or concession of the Kingdom of
Italy; because his Sovereignty bears the seal of
ages, is acknowledged by all the Powers, either
through solemn treaties, or by diplomatic relations,
which are preserved even today; and this, his right
to Sovereignty, cannot be taken away from him by
an act of pure violence." (Atti Ufficiali del Senato,
p. 769).

CHAPTER VII.

Radical defects in the Law of Guarantees.

Rejected by the Pope — The Pope the sole judge of what is necessary to secure his independence — Catholics follow his lead — The Law not sanctioned by the Powers — Negotiations fail — Italy acting in her own name — The only guarantee the word of the Pope's despoilers — The Law internal and subject to change — A narrow interpretation of its internal character — Internal laws have sometimes an international scope — Important decision of the Council of State recognizing international scope of the Law of Guarantees — The Law dependent upon a parliamentary majority — Movement for its abolition — The great obstacle — Sig. Bonghi's view — The Law more necessary to Italy than to the Pope.

The first, and obvious and radical defect of the Law of Guarantees is its non-acceptance by the Pope. The spiritual interests for which his independence is required are of a higher order than those of the State, and are beyond its control. The responsibility for those interests is concentrated in the hands of the Supreme Ruler of the Church, and no scheme of devolution can ever divest him of it. He may call others to aid him in the central

5

administration of the Church, and to share the responsibility, of which, however, they can never relieve him. He is, consequently, the ultimate judge of what is necessary to secure his independence. The great mass of catholics will be always ranged on his side, and will continue to insist on the restitution of his rights, until he assures them that he is satisfied. I shall treat of this more fully later on.

The Law of Guarantees was brought forward to solve an international question, but, as I have already stated, it has never received the sanction of the Powers. The Italian Government hoped, in the beginning, to obtain that sanction, and negotiations for the purpose were started with France and Austria. They failed, and the promulgation of the law was not even communicated to the Foreign Powers. As there was no prospect of obtaining their sanction, it was not to Italy's interest to bring it officially to their notice. As Visconti Venosta explained in his speech in the Chamber on the 20th of March 1872, " If they acknowledge the notification, they will have a right to take action with regard to that of which they have been notified. " Italy had no commission to act in the name of the Powers. She was tacitly allowed to attempt her own solution, but no approval of that solution was given. The guaranteeing power, therefore, of the Law of Guarantees is nothing more than the word of the Pope's despoilers.

A public and solemn pledge, certainly; but how many public and solemn pledges have ceased to have any restraining force when policy and expediency has suggested their violation?

It is an internal law of the Kingdom of Italy, and the power that made it can unmake it. I do not wish to push this argument for the insecurity of the law beyond due bounds, though certain isolated acts of Italy's Rulers warrant the narrowest interpretation of its internal character. After the outrage on the memory of Pius IX in July 1881, the Minister of Foreign Affairs, Sig. Mancini, sent a circular on the 27th of the same month to the Italian representatives at Foreign Courts in which he said: "You must refuse all discussion on a subject which is of a purely internal character, and affords no ground for international negotiation, and is not susceptible of international treatment." In another despatch to Berlin on the 10th of January 1882 the same Minister again affirmed "that no Italian Ministry, to whatever party it belonged, would ever allow the slightest interference in such a question, to which Italy is firmly resolved to give an aspect of a strictly internal character, as dependent solely on the national sovereignty." King Humbert, a few days later, in his address to the Chambers echoed this sentiment in the significant words: "We are, and we mean to remain, Masters in our own house. " In other words, it is no affair of other nations what treatment is meted out to the Pope by the Kingdom of Italy. This uncompromising attitude is in manifest contradiction with the many solemn assurances given by Italian Statesmen and King Victor Emmanuel II. I think it will be generally admitted that it was adopted as the sole political expedient that could save the Government in an embarrassing situation. The protest of Leo XIII against the outrage had gone forth to the world, and the Press was ringing with denunciations from all sides of the Government that could permit such a serious offence against the dignity of the Sovereign Pontiff. Either Italy was incompetent to fulfil its obligations, or unwilling, or gravely negligent. There was no satisfactory answer to be given; they resolved, therefore, to forestall any awkward questions by a stern refusal to hear them. This narrow view of Italy's obligations, which served as a temporary expedient to shield the Ministry of the day, was dropped when the special need for its use was over. The fact, however, that such a plea was ever advanced, shows on what slippery ground the law rests.

The framers of the Act itself, and Italian Statesmen generally have consistently held that, though the law is an Italian law, and imposes obligations chiefly on Italian subjects, and in Italian territory,

it has an international scope. We must recognize
that internal laws do at times give effect to international obligations, and embody in definite form
the more general ordinances of the law of nations.
The rights and liberties of foreigners are safeguarded by internal laws. Such laws, however, are on
a different basis to the ordinary prescriptions of
the national code. They may be modified, but
they cannot be entirely abrogated at the good
pleasure of the Government. Their violation may
lead to legitimate protests on the part of foreign
countries, may give rise to reprisals, and possibly
to war. In matters that do not concern the general interests of humanity, the law of nations, or
international obligations, it would be an imperti-
nence on the part of any foreign Government to
interfere.

A decision of the Italian Council of State, given
on the 2nd of March 1878, shows that the Law
of Guarantees, though an internal law, belongs to
the category of those that have an international
scope. The decision was stated in the following
terms: — " With regard to the question proposed
by the Ministry of the Interior in a note dated
19 February 1878, as to whether the Law of the
13th of May 1871, n. 214, "called of Guarantees"
forms a part of the fundamental laws of the State,
— having heard the report — the Council has con-

sidered... That this law has not the character of
an international convention, since it was spontan-
eously and freely made by the national legislative
Power, and must be regarded as an internal law
of the State... That in the task of determining
and qualifying its character and importance, if attention is paid to its origin, to the facts that pre-
ceded it and gave rise to it, to the declarations
issued with regard to it by the King's Govenment
in diplomatic documents published and laid before
Parliament, to the tenour of the reports by which
it was recommended by the Ministry to the two
branches of Parliament, and by the respective parliamentary Committees to the votes of the two
Chambers, as well as to the character of the solemn
discussion which followed, it is clear that it is an
internal law of the State, but carrying with it *ef-
fects that go beyond its confines* [*italics added*],
inasmuch as the independence of the Supreme Pontiff, the Head of Catholicity, and the free exercise
of the spiritual authority of the Holy See, which
that law insures, are a *guarantee to catholics of
every Foreign State* [*italics added*], that they will
not meet with obstacles or restraints in their relations with the Sovereign Pontiff and the Holy See...
The Commission, therefore, is of opinion that the
law of the 13th of May 1871, called " of Guarantees", is one of the most important of the internal

laws of the State, and an organic and political law, and that in the sense of the consideration heretofore laid down, may be qualified as a fundamental law of the State."

Organic and fundamental as it is, it is not immutable. It came into being by an act of Parliament, and what is to prevent Parliament from abrogating it? There has always been a current of opinion, varying in strength at different periods, among the radical sections of political parties in Italy in favour of its abolition. The liberal journal *Il Diritto* on the Ist of August 1881 wrote: — " We are in agreement with the proposal [the abolition of the Law of Guarantees]; our ideas on the question have been expressed with sufficient clearness; the ideas of the Left Party are also known; we know by inference the ideas of the Ministry, when we think of the names of some of its members — Depretis, Mancini, Zanardelli, Baccelli, Baccarini, etc.. The name of Mancini is enough by itself.

" There are well-grounded reasons, therefore, to suppose that there can be no preconception hostile to our ideas and to those of the Assembly (to promote the abolition of the law), no purpose of combating them in the parliamentary majority or among the members of the Government. Indeed, there is good reason for believing that the most pronounced Right will regard those ideas with

favour; since the Hon. Minghetti has declared his
opinion, and declared it with great precision, in his
book on the relations of the State and the Church.

" There can only be question, then, of one thing —
to choose with prudence the manner and the time
for giving to the problem the solution desired by
all. Consequently, the energies of intelligent citizens
should be directed to the facilitation of this choice. "

The radical parties of 1881 were over sanguine
in their expectations. Twenty-six years have elaps-
ed, and we are no nearer the abrogation of the
Law of Guarantees. Its permanence is not due to
its being organic and fundamental. Its special place
on the Statute Book of Italy, though it may invest
it with a privilege beyond that of many others,
purely internal laws, does not insure its perpetuity.
The obstacle to its abolition is not in the law itself,
nor in any privileged character given to it by
Italian legislators. It lies in the international character of the Papal rights which would remain even
though the law were swept entirely away. The
more prudent of Italian statesmen know that the
abrogation of the law would be the reopening of
the whole Roman Question, and the signal for the
active interference of the Foreign Powers. As
Sig. Bonghi wrote in his article on Leo XIII in the
Rassegna Nazionale of the 21st of February 1892,
" When the law is changed or ceases to be observed,

we shall lose all credit, and the day on which that
shall happen, although it is theirs to judge who
gave us the law, our pretension (to consider the
question as one of an internal character) will cease
to have any value. " It has remained untouched,
because it is needed more to protect Italian interests
than those of the Church; as far as the Pope is
concerned, were its provisions perfectly satisfactory,
the Law of Guarantees itself would stand in need
of a further guarantee, to give it that element of
stability which it lacks.

Chapter VIII.

Further defects of the Law of Guarantees.

The instability of the Law of Guarantees not a subject of complaint with the Pope — The nature of the independence offered to the Pope — No subjects, no territory — The Pope a tenant-at-will of the King of Italy — The Republic of San Marino and United Italy — The Roman Plebiscite a farce — A Plebiscite not legitimate ground for a change of dynasty — Alsace and Lorraine, Heligoland, the Federal District of Columbia — The miserable allowance set apart for the Holy See — Proposed method of payment most offensive to the Holy See.

Only a perfectly stable guarantee of Papal independence can be regarded as a satisfactory safeguard of his spiritual power, which must endure as long as the Church shall last, " even unto the consummation of the world." The Pope, however, has made no special complaint of the insecurity of the Law of Guarantees, of which I have treated in my last article. Indeed, it is one of the few satisfactory features of a most objectionable law. Were its provisions otherwise tolerable, its instability, dependent as the law is on the caprice of a parliamentary majority, would constitute a fatal flaw. But to fix unchangeably its pernicious enactments would be to rivet fast the chains it puts upon the Vicar of Christ, and to close the door against hope. The aspiration of Italian freemasons and radicals is, doubtless, to change the law for the worse, but the refusal of the Powers to sanction the Act is in harmony with the Pope's wishes, and a public attestation that a final settlement has not been reached.

What is the nature, then, of the sovereign independence which it offers to the Pope in place of the Temporal Power of which Italy has deprived him?

It gives him no subjects, as we have learnt from the Theodoli-Martinucci case, in which the Italian tribunals successfully maintained their pretension to arraign before them the Master of the Pope's household, and call the Pope to account for his treatment of his own servants in the Vatican Palace.

It allows him no territory — not even a square yard, where he can exercise sovereign rights. The Vatican Palace, and the other buildings mentioned in the fifth article of the law, are merely set aside for his use, but are regarded as the property of the Italian Crown. The Pope is a tenant-at-will of the Kingdom of Italy. The text of the article is as follows: — "The Sovereign Pontiff, besides the endowment established in the preceding article, continues to enjoy (or have the use of) [*continua a godere*] the Apostolic Palaces of the Vatican and the Lateran, with all the buildings, gardens and plots connected with them, as well as the Villa of Castel Gandolfo with all its appurtenances and dependencies. The said palaces, villas and annexes, as also the Museums, Library and artistic and archeological collections therein existent, are inalienable and exempt from all taxes or burdens, and from expropriations on any ground of public utility."

Italian Unity, it is said, demands that the whole Peninsula should be subject to Italian rule. An exception has been made in favour of the little Republic of San Marino, which forms an island in the midst of Italian territory, with autonomous government. Why should not another island exist, withdrawn from Italian jurisdiction, where the Pope might exercise the rights of a temporal Sovereign? It is not my purpose to propose any positive scheme for the settlement of the Roman Question. It is for the Pope alone to say, and to choose the time for saying, what conditions would satisfy the requirements of the Church. I am merely pointing out some obvious reasons for the Papal *Non possumus*. It was not the wish of the Roman people to be transferred to the new Kingdom of Italy. The so-called Plebiscite, which resulted in a vote of 40,785 in favour of annexation and 46 against, was a disgraceful farce. The voters were not Romans, but a rabble brought in from the provinces for the purpose. So numerous where they that many could not find lodging and were obliged to sleep out in the public squares of the City. Certificates of the right to vote and schedules with the printed "Yes" upon them were given in abundance to anybody and everybody who would receive them. Each individual was free to vote, as long as he carried an affirmative schedule, many times over in the different booths throughout the City. A young Belgian Sculptor, who wished to test the practical working of the Plebiscite, succeeded in voting as many as 22 times. Other foreigners amused themselves by going the round of the voting-stations and helping to fill the urns. The Pope called upon the Romans not to recognize the authority of the Plebiscite Committee by giving their vote.

A result adverse to the supremely important interests of the Church would be worthless, even though the Plebiscite had been conducted in a rigorously impartial manner. The consent of the inhabitants of towns and provinces is not always regarded as essential, when they are transferred from one dominion to another; otherwise, the Provinces of Alsace and Lorraine would not be German territory to-day. The fishermen of Heligoland were not consulted when they were handed over by the British Government to Prussia. In the very heart

of the most democratic of modern nations, where
representative government is carried to the extreme,
there is a strip of territory where the inhabitants
have no say in the choice of their rulers. The federal district of Columbia, where Washington, the
Capital of the United States is situated, was ceded
to Congress by the State of Maryland, so that there
might be a centre of the Union independent of all
the States. There is no parliament there, nor mu-
nicipal council, nor right of voting in presidential
elections. The people are governed by three Com-
missioners elected by Congress. It would be a small
sacrifice for Italy to make in return for the immense
advantages of reconciliation with an independent
Pope, if she gave back to him some portion of his
old territory in the supreme interests of the world-
wide Church.

What was the maintenance provided for the Holy
See when all its sources of revenue had been seized
by Italy? It is stated in the 4th article of the law,
of which the following is the text: — " There is
preserved in favour of the Holy See the endowment
of an annual revenue of 3,225,000 lire (equivalent
to 129,000 pounds sterling). With this sum, equal
to that inscribed in the Roman balance sheet under
this heading — *Sacred Apostolic Palaces, Sacred
College, Ecclesiastical Congregations, Secretariate of
State, and the Diplomatic Service abroad,* — it shall

be understood that provision has been made for the
support of the Sovereign Pontiff, and for the various
ecclesiastical needs of the Holy See, for the maintenance ordinary and extraordinary, and the custody
of the Apostolic Palaces and their dependencies;
for the assignments, and payments, and pensions
of the Guards, mentioned in the preceding article,
and of the officials of the Papal Court, and for eventual expenses; as also for the ordinary maintenance
and custody of the Museums and Library, and for
the assignments, stipends and pensions of those who
are therein employed.

The aforesaid endowment shall be inscribed in
the Great Book of the Public Debt, in the form of
perpetual and inalienable revenue in the name of
the Holy See; and during the vacancy of the Holy
See this payment will be continued to supply all
the needs peculiar to the Roman Church in this
interval.

It will be exempt from every species of tax and
State, communal or provincial burden; and it cannot
be diminished even in case the Italian Government
shall hereafter undertake the responsibility of providing for the expenses of the Museums and Library. "

One hundred and twenty-nine thousand pounds is
a small sum to cover the enormous field of expenditure here sketched out. Moreover, the expenses

of the Pope were increased by the loss of the Temporal Power. Numerous officials of the Papal Government and men on the Pontifical Army list, who had been supported out of public revenue, lost their maintenance through their loyalty to the Pope, and had to be provided for. This is naturally a dwindling item of expenditure; yet long life seems to be one of the blessings with which God has rewarded fidelity to the Vicar of Christ. A great deal of gratuitous service had been rendered in the central administration of the Church by members of Religious Orders, whose houses where suppressed and revenues confiscated by the new masters of Rome. Catholic schools had to be provided to preserve the faith of the children, which was endangered by the irreligious atmosphere of the Government schools.

The revenue offered was miserably insufficient, and the manner of its payment was most offensive to the Pope's dignity. He was not offered a capital sum which he could invest at his pleasure, and control as a free man. He was to receive his money in annual doles, and live under the perpetual fear of seeing his supplies cut off, and the machinery of ecclesiastical administration dislocated for want of means, should he incur the displeasure of his paymasters. He spurned the discreditable offer and threw himself upon the charity of the faithful.

6

Chapter IX.

Diplomatic Relations and Pontifical Acts under the Law.

Text of the Law on Diplomatic Relations with the Holy See
— Permanent relations between the Holy See and Foreign
Powers — Occasional missions — These relations not due
to a concession of the Law — Italy cannot abolish them,
nor control them in time of peace — The Pope's freedom
of communication curtailed in time of war — Supreme
interests of the Church dependent on the good-will of
Italy — Publication of Papal Acts allowed to ecclesiastics,
their approval liable to punishment — General review of
the Law — Its sovereignty a mockery.

The 11th article of the Law of Guarantees provides for the free communication of Foreign Governments with the Holy See, and *viceversa*. It runs
as follows: — " The Envoys of Foreign Governments to His Holiness enjoy in the Kingdom all
the prerogatives and immunities which belong to
Diplomatic Agents according to International Law.

" To offences against them are extended the penal
sanctions for offences against the Envoys of Foreign Powers to the Italian Government. To the
Envoys of His Holiness to Foreign Governments
are assured, in the territory of the Kingdom, the

customary prerogatives and immunities, according to the same Law, in going to and returning from the place of their mission."

The Holy See is at present in permanent diplomatic relations with various Governments, through Apostolic Nuncios, Internuncios, or Apostolic Delegates and Envoys Extraordinary resident at the foreign seats of Government, or through Ambassadors or Ministers resident at Rome, or by reciprocal representation at Rome and abroad. Foreign Governments represented by Ambassadors at the Papal Court are: — Austria-Hungary, Spain and Portugal. Those represented by Envoys Extraordinary and Plenipotentiary Ministers are: — Bavaria, Belgium, Bolivia, Brasil, Chili, Columbia, Costarica, San Domingo, Haiti, Monaco, Nicaragua, Peru, Prussia, Russia and the Argentine Republic is at present represented at the Vatican by a Chargé d'Affaires. The Holy See is represented with the following Governments: — by Apostolic Nuncios of the first class in Austria-Hungary, Spain and Portugal; by Apostolic Nuncios of the second class in Bavaria, Belgium and Brasil; by an Internuncio at Buenos Ayres with the Argentine Republic, Uruguay and Paraguay; by Delegates Apostolic and Envoys Extraordinary in Chili, Columbia, Equador, Bolivia and Peru, San Domingo, Haiti and Venezuela; in Holland and Luxemburg by Chargés d'Affaires.

Other Powers have sent occasional missions to the Holy See to treat questions of special interest to them. Sir Lintorn Simmons was sent by England to negotiate with the Holy See matters connected with Malta, and Mr. Taft a few years ago treated in the name of the United States with Leo XIII concerning questions of ecclesiastical property in the Philippines. Leo XIII acted as arbitrator between Germany and Spain, at the request of those two Powers, in the question of the Caroline Islands. Queen Victoria sent the Duke of Norfolk as her representative with an autograph letter to Leo XIII on the occasion of his Sacerdotal Jubilee in 1887, and, at another Jubilee celebration of the same Pontiff, Lord Denbigh represented King Edward VII.

I need not enlarge on the importance which various Powers, catholic and non-catholic, place upon the maintenance of diplomatic relations with the Holy See, nor on the necessity of protecting the confidential character of such relations with the usual safeguards of secrecy. It was a prudent measure on the part of Italian Statesmen to introduce into the Law of Guarantees a clause providing for the extra-territoriality of the residences of Envoys to the Holy See. But what would have been the situation, supposing that clause had been omitted? Precisely the same as that which exists at present. Would the German Emperor, for in-

stance, refrain from establishing a Legation at the
Vatican, because Italy had failed to declare in the
Law of Guarantees that Foreign Governments were
free to conduct diplomatic relations with the Sovereign Pontiff? Would the same Emperor look on
with indifference, or without protest, if the Italian
Government happened to order a perquisition in
the house of his Minister on some pretext of judicial enquiry, or for State reasons? The hand of Italy
is held, not so much out of respect for its own law,
as out of consideration for international obligations,
and from fear of the consequences of their violation.
Strong Powers could enforce their right, and even
weaker Powers might embarrass with reprisals.
This clause of the Law of Guarantees confers no
new right on Foreign Powers or on the Holy See.
International law and usage gives the right of in-
tercommunication by means of Legations between
the Powers and the Holy See, and exacts the privilege of extra-territoriality of these Legations as
the only means of protecting the confidential nature
of their charge. Italy, it is true, seems to be protecting in what it looks upon as its own territory
embassies to one who under actual conditions may
be described as in some sense Italy's enemy. On
the other hand, we must remember that Italy was
fully aware that in taking possession of Rome, she
was establishing her sway over a territory that must

be encumbered with such servitudes, if international
rights were to be respected. And should she pro-
claim the incompatibility of such servitudes with
her own vital interests, it would only be a proof
that by her invasion of Rome she had brought about
a situation that necessarily deprives the Sovereign
Pontiff of freedom and independence in the government of the Church.

There is one contingency for which no provision
is made in the Law of Guarantees, — the eventuality
of war between Italy and some other Power. Si-
gnor Corte, a member of the Italian Parliament, in
the sitting of the 15th of February 1871, proposed
an amendment, declaring that all the privileges
accorded to the Pope with respect to Ambassadors
accredited to the Vatican, and to the despatch of
telegrams and correspondence, should be suspended
in case of war between Italy and other nations, as
also in the case of war between other peoples, when
Italy had declared herself neutral, and in every cir-
cumstance when such a measure should be necessary for the internal and external security of the
State. Sig. Bonghi accepted the amendment, but
refused to embody it in the law, on the ground
that this was concerned merely with the rights or
peace, and not those of war. In time of war, then,
Italy would expel from Rome the staff of any em-
bassy accredited to the Holy See, that belonged to

a hostile Power. The correspondence of the Holy See would be submitted to a rigorous control. Were the Pope in possession of his own little State, he could communicate freely with belligerent countries; his freedom of communication with them in the future is conditioned by the view which the Italian Government takes of any war that may be waged. Intercourse between the Sovereign Pontiff and any Power with which Italy happened to be at war, would be rendered impossible. Italy is not to be blamed for taking every precaution to ensure the success of her arms in war; she cannot, however, at the same time claim that she has left the Pope free and independent in his spiritual rule. His fortunes are henceforth, according to the Italian view, bound up with those of his conqueror, and the supreme interests of the Church must depend in certain contingencies on the good-will of Italy.

Article 10 of the Law provides for the publication of Pontifical Decrees: — " Ecclesiastics, who by reason of their office share in the issue in Rome of the Acts of the Spiritual Ministry of the Holy See, are not liable by reason of the same to any molestation, enquiry, or control of the Public Authority. Every foreigner invested with an ecclesiastical office in Rome, enjoys the personal guarantees belonging to Italian citizens in virtue of the law of the Kingdom. " If the Papal decree is in

opposition to Italian Law, its publication by a layman would render him liable to punishment. Only
official publication by ecclesiastics is protected and
nothing more. If ecclesiastic or layman ventures
to execute such a decree, or express approval of
it, they must bear the full responsibility of their
acts before the Italian tribunals. The catholic Press
of Rome has had ample experience of its unpro-
tected condition in the sequestration of journals,
the imposition of fines and imprisonment for simple
comment on and loyal acceptance of Papal decrees.

From the foregoing cursory review of the Law
of Guarantees we have seen that, while giving to
the Pope a sovereign designation, it leaves him
without territory and without subjects, — a form
of sovereignty hitherto unknown in the world. The
paradoxical suggestion has been made that the
condition of the Pope is that of a Sovereign on
foreign travel. The one Sovereign on the whole
earth, whom the iron necessity of the case keeps
shut up within the walls of his own palace, a Sovereign on foreign travel! The Law, again, would
place the Sovereign Pontiff in the humiliating position of a salaried official of the Kingdom of Italy,
with a miserable pittance, totally inadequate to the
needs of his spiritual government. It curtails in
many ways his independence in the discharge of his
responsible office, and hampers his freedom of com-

munication with foreign countries. In the strong
words of the French liberal statesman, Emile Ollivier, a Minister of Napoleon III, — " The Guarantees make of the Pope a subject of the King, and
of the Papacy a department of the internal administration of the Kingdom of Italy. " (*Le Pape, est-il
libre à Rome?* par Emile Ollivier de l'Académie
française). In the same work (p. 12) he says: —
" If it has seemed hitherto that the Guarantees
have shown some measure of solidity, it was only
because they were never applied. They have hin-
dered collisions for over ten years, because they
did not allow encounters; the two parties never
came to blows, because they were never face to
face; there were no false steps, because one of the
combatants never moved. The Guarantees, therefore, are of no use, unless they are not used; they
will end in smoke when the Pope ventures to show
himself in the streets of Rome. They may be
compared, in fact, to a railroad on which no di-
sasters have yet occurred, because no train has
passed over it. "

The sovereignty of the Law of Guarantees is
not real. We cannot wonder that Pius IX called
it a mockery (*ludibrium*), and likened it to the
scarlet cloak thrown about the shoulders of Christ
in the Hall of Pilate.

Chapter X.

The Papal Protest.

The protest continuous since 1870 — The principle involved — Encyclical of Pius IX, May 15, 1870 — Leo XIII repeats the *non possumus* — The olive branch in the Allocution of May 23, 1887 — Important letter of Leo XIII to his Secretary of State, June 15, 1887 — Cardinal Rampolla's letter to the Pontifical Nuncios, June 22, 1887 — Accession of Pius X — His antecedents and character — His first Allocution — Letter of his Secretary of State concerning the visit of M. Loubet to Rome.

The protest of the Popes against the Law of Guarantees has been strong and continuous from the year 1870 till the present time. It has been made in the uncompromising attitude which they have studiously maintained towards the King of Italy and the Italian Government, in weighty utterances on many solemn occasions, in public addresses to the Sacred College of Cardinals, in letters to Apostolic Nuncios, and in Encyclicals addressed to the Bishops of the whole Church. The principle laid down is always the same. The position of the Pope as Head of the Universal Church requires

that he should be free and independent in the exercise of his Apostolic Ministry, and that his freedom and independence should be manifest to the whole world. Such freedom and independence can only be secured by a real and effective sovereignty; the sovereignty offered by the Law of Guarantees is not real and effective, and the position it creates for the Pope is one of subjection.

Two days after the passing of the Law, on May the 15th 1870, Pius IX issued his first Encyclical of protest, from which I make the following quotation: "Although the Faithful committed to your charge have already openly expressed by letters or by most weighty documents of protest their indignation at the oppression of which We are the victims, and shown how little they are deluded by the deceits veiled under the name of guarantees, nevertheless we consider it a duty of our Apostolic office to declare solemnly to the whole world through you that not only the dispositions called the *Guarantees*, but also the titles, honours, immunities and privileges, whatever they may be, which are included in the name of guarantees, are absolutely incapable of securing the unfettered and free use of our divinely-given power, and of safeguarding the essential liberty of the Church.

"Under these circumstances, therefore, as We have many times declared and professed that We cannot, without sinfully violating the oath by which We are bound, agree to any compromise that will destroy our rights, or curtail the divine rights of the Apostolic See; so now, by virtue of our office, We declare that We shall never, nor can We ever, admit or accept the guarantees invented by the Subalpine Government, whatever may be their character, nor any other conditions of the sort, whatever may be their nature or sanction, which under pretext of safeguarding our sacred power and liberty are offered to Us in place of and as a substitute for that Civil Principality, with which divine Providence willed the Holy See to be endowed and fortified, and which rests upon legitimate and unassailable titles, as well as on the actual possession for over eleven hundred years. It must be plain to any one that if the Roman Pontiff is subject to the sway of another Sovereign, he can be no longer possessed of supreme power in the political order, nor would he be able, whether his own person or the acts of his Apostolic Ministry be considered, to free himself from the control of the one to whom he would be subject, and who might turn out to be a heretic or a persecutor of the Church, or be engaged in war with other Sovereigns, or be in a state of civil war.

" Moreover, is not this concession of the guarantees, of which We speak, a most clear proof in itself, that laws are imposed upon Us, to whom has been given by God the power of legislating in the moral and religious order, and who have been appointed interpreters of the natural and divine law for the whole earth, and that these imposed laws regard the government of the Universal Church, and depend for their preservation and their working entirely upon what the lay powers may please to prescribe and decree?

" As regards the relation of the Church towards Civil Society, you know well, Venerable Brethren, that we have received directly from God Himself in the person of Blessed Peter all the prerogatives and all the rights of authority necessary to rule the Universal Church, and further, that these prerogatives and rights, as the freedom itself of the Church, are the object and the offspring of the blood-shedding of Jesus Christ, and must be valued according to the infinite price of this Divine Blood. We should deserve very ill, therefore, of the Divine Blood of our Redeemer, which God forbid, were We to accept from the Rulers of the earth these rights of ours, which at this particular time they would hand over to Us in a retrenched and perverted form. For Christian Rulers are not masters of the Church, but sons; Anselm, Archbishop of Canterbury, that beacon of holiness and learning, gave them the following appropriate injunction: – 'Remember that the Church

of God has not been given to you as to a master
who can command its service, but has been com-
mended to you as to an advocate and defender:
God loves nothing in this world more than the
liberty of His Church (Ep. 8 lib. IV).' And in
another place he exhorts them in these words: 'Do
not consider that the dignity of your exalted position suffers if you love and defend the liberty of
the Spouse of God and of your Mother the Church;
do not imagine that you are humbled if you exalt
her; do not think that you are weakened if you
strengthen her. Look around you and see; instances
are not far to seek; consider the Rulers who attack
her and trample upon her – what is their gain, and
what is the upshot? It is clear enough and needs
no setting forth. Without any doubt they who glorify
her will be glorified with her and in her (Ep. 12,
lib. IV).'

" Wherefore, it is evident to everybody as We
have declared to you, Venerable Brethren, on this
and other occasions, that the injury done to the
Holy See in these disastrous times is felt throughout
the whole of Christendom. As St Bernard says,
an offence against the Apostles, those glorious
Princes of the earth, touches every Christian; and
as the Church of Rome, as the above-mentioned
St Anselm used to say, labours for all the churches,
whoever takes away her rights, is convicted of

sacrilege not only against her, but against all the churches. And, indeed, there can be no doubt in the mind of any one that the preservation of the rights of this Apostolic See is intimately united and bound up with the highest interests and advantages of the Universal Church and with the liberty of your own Episcopal ministry. "

It might be thought that the protest of Pius IX was due to his sense of the personal wrong he had suffered, and to his inability in his old age to adapt himself to altered circumstances. But Leo XIII, who had never enjoyed the civil authority, repeated the *non possumus* of his predecessor, and repeated it to the end. He had seen the labours of his long Pontificate crowned with success in every part of the world; he had received the homage of all peoples in a magnificent demonstration thrice renewed in his triple jubilee; in the opinion of those who are outside the Church he was preeminently a man of peace and conciliation; he seemed to belong more to the other world than to the one in which he ruled; if ever there was a time and an occasion and a man, that combined to favour the utterance of the word of peace, it was when all the nations were gathered in respect and veneration round the white figure of the aged Pontiff in his latest jubilee. If Leo XIII refused to declare peace, and continued his protest and his cry of *non possumus*, it is evident that he was swayed by motives higher than any earthly considerations.

As far back as the year 1887, in an important Allocution delivered on the 23rd of May, he held out the olive branch to Italy, and manifested his desire of peace on tolerable conditions. " Would that the desire of pacification ", he said, " which We feel for all peoples, could profit Italy, which God has joined with such close bonds to the Roman Pontificate, and which by the very instinct of nature is most dear to Us. We, indeed, as We have often said, have long and earnestly desired that the minds of Italians should enjoy security and peace, and the disastrous conflict with the Roman Pontificate should at last come to an end; but with the preservation of justice and the dignity of the Apostolic See, which have been violated, not so much by the lawless action of the people, as by the conspiracy of the sects. The way to concord, then, must be in that condition of things, in which the Roman Pontiff is subject to no one, and enjoys a full and true liberty, as every right demands. From this fact, if rightly viewed, no harm could come to the interests of Italy, but rather an increase of her security and prosperity. ,,

His advances were repulsed, and his words wilfully misconstrued. In a letter to his newly-ap-

7

pointed Cardinal Secretary of State, Cardinal Rampolla, on June the 15th of the same year 1887, he
makes a general review of the position of the Holy
See with regard to Foreign Powers, and deals at
length with the question of his independence.
" Many times, " he writes, " have We expressed
our desire to see this conflict finally settled; and
also recently, in the Consistorial Allocution of the
23rd of May last, We declared our wish to extend
the work of pacification, as to other countries, so
also in an especial way to Italy, so dear to Us and
so intimately allied to Us on many grounds. Here,
however, in order to establish concord, it is not
enough, as elsewhere, to provide for some religious
interest in particular, to modify or abrogate hostile
laws, to forestall impending measures, but it is necessary besides and above all to regulate in a
proper manner the condition of the Supreme Head
of the Church, which for many years through violence and injustice has been unworthy of him, and
incompatible with the liberty of the Apostolic office. Therefore, in the aforesaid Allocution, We
took care to lay down as the foundation of this
pacification justice and the dignity of the Apostolic
See, and to claim for Ourselves a state of things,
in which the Roman Pontiff shall be subject to no
one, and enjoy liberty full and unfeigned. There
was no ground for the misconstruction of our words,

and much less for the perversion and the distor-
tion of their meaning to something quite opposed
to our thought. They bore unmistakeably the
sense intended by Us, namely, that an indispensable condition for pacification in Italy is to give
to the Roman Pontiff a true sovereignty. Since
*in the present state of things We are more in the
power of others, than in our own* [*italics added*];
and upon their will it rests to change, when and
how they please, according to the variation of men
and circumstances, the very conditions of our existence. Therefore, have We always, in the course
of our Pontificate, as was our duty, claimed for the
Roman Pontiff an effective sovereignty, not through
ambition, or with a view to earthly greatness, but
as a real and effective safeguard of his independence and liberty...

" From all this it is easy to understand how the
obligation is imposed upon the Roman Pontiffs,
and how sacred for them is the duty, of defending
and maintaining civil sovereignty and the ground
on which it rests; a duty rendered still more sacred
by the bond of an oath. It would be folly to pre-
tend that they themselves agreed to sacrifice with
civil sovereignty that which they hold most dear
and precious; we mean their own liberty to govern
the Church, for which their predecessors have on
every occasion so gloriously fought.

" We shall certainly, with the help of God, not fail in our duty, and except by a return to a true and effective sovereignty, such as is required by our independence and the dignity of the Apostolic See, We see no other way open to agreement and peace. The whole of the catholic world, jealous in the last degree of the liberty of its Head, will not rest until it sees his just claims satisfied. "

A week later, on the 22nd of June 1887, the Cardinal Secretary of State returns to the same argument in his letter to the Pontifical Nuncios at Foreign Courts. " ...It is not true, " he writes, " that independence in the free government of the Church and the dignity of the Sovereign Pontiff would be secured, as is required, without the guarantee, the sole effective guarantee, of territorial sovereignty.

" Great sagacity is not needed to understand that the Sovereign Pontiff, deprived in his See of his own true territorial sovereignty, will always be the subject and the guest of another, solely and principally sovereign; consequently, whatever appearance of liberty and independence should be accorded by this power under any sort of form, besides being legally revocable by the power which gave it, would always be liable to infraction and illusory...

" The Pope, not being a Sovereign in his own See, would find himself continually thrust into humiliating situations, unbecoming the sublimity of his position.

" He would, moreover, be obliged to have as servants, counsellors, coadjutors and cooperators of every kind, indispensable in the exercise of his Apostolic Ministry, persons subject to the extraneous authority of another Ruler.

" From all that precedes it is easy to conclude that neither justice, nor the independence, nor the dignity itself of the Supreme Pontiff, could be preserved if Italy should persist in retaining the spoils of the temporal dominion, to the grievous injury of the Holy Apostolic See. "

When Pius X came to the throne, hopes were entertained by Italian Liberals that now at last the *intransigeance* of the Vatican would come to an end. Here was a man of the people, who knew their aspirations, in the Chair of Peter. He was not a native of the old Pontifical States, and had never lived within its borders. He belonged to the Venetian Province, whence as a young man he had seen the Austrians driven out by men of his own blood. He had stood on platforms with members of the reigning House of Savoy, had shown them honour, and been honoured by them in return. His mind was not prejudiced by traditions of ecclesiastical diplomacy. Without earthly ambitions, the passion of his life was the spiritual interests of his flock and of the Church of Christ, and the practice of charity to all men. His character and antecedents, the whole tenour of his simple, self-sacrificing, austere life put it beyond doubt that he could not pose for dramatic effect, or exhibit his chains to win sympathy, or be swayed by any petty motive of resentment at the diminution of the temporal prestige and power of the Papacy. Yet he took up at once the same attitude of protest as his Predecessors. In his first Allocution to the Sacred College on the 9th of November 1903 he said: — " Since it is necessary and of the highest importance to Christendom that the Pope in the government of the Church should be, and appear to be, free and independent of any power, therefore, as our duty demands, and the sacred obligation of the oath by which We are bound, We complain that a most grievous injury has been done the Church in this respect. "

When the President of the French Republic broke the tradition of reserve till then maintained by the Heads of all Catholic States, the Papal Secretary of State, Cardinal Merry Del Val, wrote thus to the French Ambassador, M. Nisard, on the 28th of April 1904: — " Consequently, if the Head of any Catholic nation grievously offends the Sovereign Pontiff, by coming to pay homage at Rome, that is to say, in the very Seat of the Pontiff, and even in his Apostolic Palace, *to him who, contrary to all right, retains his Civil Principality, and fetters his freedom and necessary independence* [*italics added*], this offence has been far greater on the part of M. Loubet. "

CHAPTER XI.

The Moral Power of the Papacy.

A luminous fact, a specious argument and a false inference
— The Church triumphs in spite of persecutors, not
because of them — The Pope's sacrifice — The Pope
a prisoner, not a slave — The hypothesis of the Law of
Guarantees — Consequent distrust and suspicion — The
danger of Italian nationalism in the counsels of the Church
— The state of protest of the Holy See a guarantee to
the Catholic world.

I must now deal with one imporant consideration
which, to some minds, seems to weaken the force
of the Papal protest. It is the luminous fact that
the moral power of the Papacy was never greater
than it is now, and has been for the last twenty
or thirty years, The false inference is too readily
drawn that this is due to the disappearance of the
Temporal Power. " Why, then, " it is urged, " shed
fruitless tears over a mere civil appanage that is
irrevocably gone? The Pope is in reality greater
than ever he was; his position is ideal — a spiritual
Ruler ruling the spirits of men. His power is seen
to be truly divine, when it is divorced from every

semblance of earthly away. Restoration to temporal
power would only add to his embarrassments without
contributing one jot to his moral influence which, in
the words of King Edward VII spoken of Leo XIII,
' makes itself felt far beyond the bounds of the
Church of which he is the exalted Head. ' "

This argument *ad hominem* has been used by
unbelievers and enemies of the Church, who would
gladly see Papal dominion of any kind, spiritual as
well as temporal, entirely abolished. But even sin-
cere catholics, who have given only a superficial
consideration to the many factors in the situation,
have been unduly impressed by its force. Italian
Liberals, surprised at a result beyond their previ-
sions, have sometimes boldly taken credit to themselves for strengthening the Church by ridding it
of secular cares. They have, forsooth, stripped it
of the cumbersome armour, unsuited to its limbs,
and left it with its sling and pebbles and its faith
in the Giver of victories. Could the Emperor Nero
revisit Rome, he might with equal justice make a
similar boast. Imagine the spectre of the cruel
despot surveying from the summit of the Palatine
Hill the scene where he once ruled. As he looks
to the Esquiline he can hardly perceive a trace of
his Golden Palace on which he squandered the imperial treasures. At his feet is a crumbling mass
of ruins, the remains of the once magnificent Pala-

ces of the Caesars. It was in one of those halls
that Peter the Fisherman was tried and condemned
to death. And across the Tiber rises the mighty
dome that marks the spot where the Apostle's
hallowed remains were enshrined — the goal of
reverent pilgrims from every land through the ages.
But who gave the first Vicar of Christ the halo of
martyrdom but Nero? The blood of the martyrs
was the seed of this powerful Church which has
encompassed the earth, outlasted by many centuries
the Empire of Rome, and gives promise to see the
world's end. But who ever cast this fertile seed
on the fields of Roman dominion with more un-
sparing hand than Nero?

The Church has thriven in this latest persecution,
as it has thriven before, not from the blows of its
enemies, but from its own innate, God-given vigour.
Divine Providence has drawn good out of evil.
Undoubtedly the moral power of the Papacy shines
with an added splendour from the contrast of the
spoliation of which he is the victim. By the sacrifice
of his individual liberty and his refusal to jeopardize
the interests of the Church by submission to the
Italian Government, the Pope has preserved his
honour untarnished, his dignity intact, and the
Church free from servitude. He is, indeed, a prisoner,
but not a slave, as the Law of Guarantees would
make him. And that he is free from real or ap-

parent slavery is clear to the world from the very
fact that he lives in a state of protest against the
Power at his door.

But let us suppose another state of things, — that,
namely, contemplated by the Italian Law. Let us suppose that he is living on terms of peace and friendship, and in friendly intercourse with the Italian Government, and interpret in the light of this fact
some of his Pontifical acts. Leo XIII is credited
with a victory over Bismarck, the iron Chancellor
of Germany, by forcing the repeal of the Falck
Laws. But all the efforts of the Centre Party under
the leadership of Windthorst might have been in
vain, if the Chancellor could have said to the German
people. — " It is unworthy of a great Empire like
ours to sacrifice its interests at the bidding of one
who is serving the King of Italy. " The same Pope
called upon Frenchmen, whether Royalists or Bona-
partists or Nationalists, to rally to the Republic
and leave aside their contentions to serve their
country and the Church. But Frenchmen might
easily have regarded this Papal act as a decree
issued at the instigation of the Italian Government,
with whom they were not at the time on friendly
terms. In fact, whenever the Pope should happen
to raise his voice on matters of public and prime
importance within the bounds of a foreign Kingdom,
sinister interpretations would be given; the hand

of Italy would be seen, and distrust and suspicion
of the Supreme Pastor would be fostered in the
minds of the faithful. A handle would be given
for calumnious reports even where there was little
ground, and it would be extremely difficult to dis-
prove them. The bonds of allegiance between the
faithful and their Head would be weakened. So
Pius IX said in his Allocution of April 20, 1849,
which I have already quoted : — " Peoples, Kings
and Nations would never turn with free confidence
and devotion to the Bishop of Rome, if they saw
him the subject of the Sovereign and the Government in whose territory he dwelt. And under
this pretext the decrees of the Pontiff would oftentimes be disobeyed. "

Ill-founded suspicion, moreover, is not the only
danger to be guarded against. There is another
hypothesis which we must regard as possible. And
that is, that the Pope would on some occasions
yield to the pressure of the Government on which
he depended, and with which he lived on terms
of intimacy. Happily, the Church during the last
century has been blessed with Pontiffs of sterling
character, men high-minded, prudent and strong-
willed, who were not likely to be led out of the
true path by undue persuasion, or terrified by the
menace of hardships and privations. But there is
no divine promise that the individuals who sit in

the Chair of Peter will always be worthy of the
high office which they are called upon to fill. The
grave interests of the Church cannot be allowed
to depend for their normal condition on the heroic
character of its Pontiffs. By their very position
should they be raised not only above suspicion, but
above temptation in their pastoral office. We can
easily imagine what insistent, insidious, over-ruling
forms such a temptation might assume. Picture the
situation created by the acceptance on the part of
the Pope of the political expedient of the Law of
Guarantees, offered to him by the Italian Government. There would naturally ensue, not merely
an interchange of courtesies, but a certain inter-
mingling of the two Courts. The Pope's own
counsellors would be seen in the halls of the Quirinal, and in the houses of Ministers and supporters
of a possibly unscrupulous Government; they would
be surrounded by an atmosphere of Italian nationalism; their love of their native land, their concern
for its welfare, and perhaps the motive of self-
interest, would dispose them insensibly to accept
the official Italian view of grave matters of ecclesiastical policy. To the direct pressure of the
Italian Government on the Pope would be added
the urgent advice of his own counsellors imbued
with the ideas of Italian officialdom, and matters
in which the Pontiff dared not act on his own

unaided judgment, would be settled with a view
to the interests of Italy and not those of the Universal Church. What sort of reception would a
Pontifical utterance, which touched on the borderland
of religion and politics, receive in another country,
when it became known or suspected that it was
manufactured in the Italian Cabinet? We can realize
the sarcastic comments of the Press, and the scandal
of the faithful. " The Pope, " it would be said,
" is the creature of the Quirinal, the Head Chaplain
of the House of Savoy. The message is delivered
by the Pope; but it was given to him by Italy's
King, the Pope's paymaster. " Papal instructions,
that offended the susceptibilities of a foreign Government that was not on good terms with Italy,
would be pointed to as a counter-stroke of an Italian
Minister. The Vatican would come to be looked
upon as a department of the Italian Foreign Office.

Such charges are not made now, and why?
Simply because of the aloofness, the separation of
the Vatican from the Quirinal. Its state of protest
and hostility to the Italian Monarchy at its doors
is a guarantee to the nations that the Holy See
regards the interests of the Church with a single
eye. The rigourous etiquette, that forbids any
guest of the King of Italy to go straight from the
Palace of the Quirinal to the presence of the Pope,
is part of the general policy of closing up the

avenues against the approach of national influence into the spiritual domain of the Church. The seeming peace to be bought by an alliance with United Italy on the terms which it offers would be the sure harbinger of decay. Far better is it that the Pope should be a prisoner in the Vatican in the possession of the confidence of the catholic world, than enjoy a freedom of subjection with the distrust and suspicion of catholics in other lands. Peace on the conditions offered by the Law of Guarantees would make the last state of the Holy See worse than the first. In the words of the Italian proverb, "si stava meglio quando si stava peggio." It were better that the Pope were imprisoned in a fortress, isolated from his advisers and the Bishops of the Church, as Pius VII was at Fontainebleau, than enjoy a freedom from material restraint which laid daily and hourly snares to prostitute his spiritual pre-eminence to the petty aims of some national ambition. The gross, personal outrage could only be of short duration, and would not give his captors control of his spiritual power. But the systematic bondage implied in the surrender of his claims would be difficult to throw off, and would go far to neutralize his influence over the world-wide Church.

Chapter XII.

The Actual Situation.

The Pope continues exercise of sovereign rights — In his
last stronghold — The armed truce — The drawbacks to
Italy, to Foreign Powers and to the Holy See — Italy
assailed with Catholic protests — Disturbing incidents —
The diplomatic see-saw — Latter of the Empress of Austria
— The *non expedit.* — The Vicar of Christ the sole
judge — The Duke of Nofrolk and the Catholic Union of
Great Britain.

Though the Pope has rejected the Law of
Guarantees with all its pretended concessions of
rights, privileges, and immunities, he continues to
maintain the rank and style of an independent
Sovereign, and to exercise Sovereign rights within
the limitations imposed by the armed occupation
of the whole of his old territory except that little
foothold, where he lives a moral prisoner. His own
standard, with the tiara and crosskeys, floats over
the Vatican. The Swiss Guard in antique costume,
that keep watch at the entrance of his palace, carry
our minds back four hundred years to the warrior
Pope Julius II, under whose reign they were first

8

formed. As the body-guard of the Pope, they are fulfilling the same duties today as they have done for centuries. These with the Noble Guard, the Gendarmes and the Palatine Guard, are not merely armed servants; but real soldiers, not bound by any oath of allegiance to the King of Italy, obedient only to the orders of the Pope. No Italian uniform is ever seen inside the Vatican. Even the humble postman appears without braid and brass buttons, in simple civilian dress, when he delivers the Vatican post. Certificates of births and deaths within the Vatican area given by the Papal doctors are regarded as authentic by the Italian authorities, without further formalities; the Italian tribunals accept as valid the processes of magisterial enquiry into cases of criminals, who might take refuge within its walls, according to the usual international forms. The Sovereign Pontiff continues to bestow titles of nobility, knightly orders, and decorations. He preserves diplomatic relations with foreign States without any reference to the Italian Government.

All these distinctive attributes of sovereignty the Pope has continued to exercise, as in the centuries that are past, on the indisputable title of lawful possession for over eleven hundred years. The military surrender of Rome to the overwhelming forces of the enemy placed the Eternal City in their power, except that portion in the immediate

neighbourhood of the Vatican, between the bastions
of Santo Spirito and the Castle of S. Angelo, which
was specially excluded in the terms of capitulation.
Into this district the Italians were afterwards called
by the Pope himself to preserve order, as the crush-
ing blow he had received left him unable to cope
with the disorderly rabble that followed on the
heels of the invading army. The Italian troops
advanced no farther. They have never ventured
to cross the threshold of the Vatican, where, as in
his last stronghold, the Pope since 1870 has remained entrenched. It matters little what motive
caused them to refrain from dealing this final blow,
— whether from fear of catholic opinion throughout
the world, of the international complications that
might follow, or from dread of the departure from
Rome of the Pope, who might cause more trouble
from abroad than he could in their midst. The
fact remains that the blow has not fallen, and the
Pope retains in his last refuge whatever elements of
sovereignty the unfinished conquest has left him.
No treaty of peace followed the cessation of hosti-
lities; the Pope has signed away none of his rights;
and for thirty seven years the belligerents have
stood face to face under the conditions of an armed
truce.

This state of suspended warfare is fraught with
drawbacks for Italy as well as for the Holy See,

and is a continual source of embarrassment to other
Powers. Foreign States, in their position as neut-
rals, can espouse neither one side nor the other.
They may be relied upon to prevent any assembly
of armed forces in their territory, or recruiting of
soldiers among their subjects to make war upon
Italy. But, on the other hand, as the Roman
Question is still open, they must allow their catholic
subjects full freedom to associate themselves with
their Spiritual Chief in his protest against the intol-
erable position in which he is placed. So year
after year Italy has had to put up, as best it might,
with the vehement condemnation of its oppression
of the Pope, delivered in almost all lands at Catholic
Congresses, in the Press. in published pastorals,
and even in national Parliaments. The oft-repeated
cry of " *Roma Intangibile*" only testifies to the
strength and persistence of the opposing sentiment,
of which it is a defiance. If, smarting under the
denunciations uttered against her in other countries,
Italy remonstrates with the Ruling Powers, she is
forced to be satisfied with some formula of smooth
words, which leaves the offence unpunished and
the offenders free to repeat it. Even this meagre
satisfaction may be neutralized by a corresponding
official note despatched to the Holy See. In his
celebrated Pastoral on the incidents of the funeral of
Pius IX on the 13th of July 1881, the Arch

bishop of Toledo, Cardinal Moreno, had said: " Either
the Italian Government did not know how, or was
unable, or unwilling to prevent them, and in any of
these hypotheses it is impossible for the Pontiff to
go on thus at the mercy of a Power which tolerated
such scandals. " The Italian Minister at Madrid
pressed for the prohibition of the Pastoral. His
Government, however, had to express itself satisfied
with a telegram, despatched on the 3rd of August
by the Spauish Government, in which it declared
its displeasure that a Spanish Prelate should mix
up in affairs outside his ministry, "hoping that this
candid manifestation and the sincerity with which
the Spanish Government proposed to continue its
international relations with the Italian King and
people, with whom it desired to draw still closer,
if it were possible, the bonds of friendship, would
be looked upon as a conclusive proof of its real
sentiments· " On the very same date of the 3rd of
August, the Spanish Government sent the following
message to the Papal Nuncio, " Anything which
gives pain to the Holy Pather is a cause of grief
to the Government, and it takes this opportunity
of renewing to Your Excellency the expression of
the profound respect and high esteem it has for
the Common Father of the faithful . . . . , but it is
necessary to reconcile its filial adhesion to the
Catholic Church with the duties which International

Law imposes upon peoples, duties which the Spanish people fulfils as best it can, without thereby ceasing to profess the deepest veneration for the August Pontiff, who rules today the destinies of Catholicism (Red Book, 1881). "

Another similar incident in Spanish diplomacy in the year 1884 is narrated by the Marquis de Olivart, together with the preceding one, in his excellent work on the juridical aspect of the Roman Question, entiled: " Il Papa, Gli Stati della Chiesa e l'Italia " (Italian edition, Gianini & Sons, Naples, 1601). Mr Pidal was taunted with the renunciation of his principles by taking office in a Cabinet which boasted of its friendship with Italy. He rebutted the charge iu a fervid oration, in which the expressions of his loyal attachment to the Holy See were, perhaps, exaggerated by the Press. The Quirinal demanded an explanation, and it was replied that the scope of the parliamentary discussion had been confined to the personal religious and political views of Mr Pidal. The Italian Government thought to improve the occasion by prefixing an historical resumé of the incident to the publication of the correspondence, giving to understand that a real agreement had been arrived at, in which Mr Elduayen had formally declared that "nobody in Spain ever discusses now the question of the Temporal Power, which was no longer an object of controversy either directly or indirectly, and that the possession of Rome by Italy was as legitimate as that of Alsace and Lorraine or of Gibraltar, being confirmed as those were, by the public European Law in force. " The Holy See now made remonstrances, expressing the astonishment caused by such words, finding these sentiments of his Ministers, expressing solidarity with the sacrilegious and violent spoliation, incompatible with the principles always maintained by His Majesty's Government. Ample and satisfactory explanations were given to the Holy See, in which it was clearly stated that Spain gave no sanction to acts towards which she had in no wise contributed, nor sought to contribute, nor could she give to them her approval much less her support. The only thing that the Minister of State could say was that Spain, as a Government, was not discussing at that moment the Roman Question, and was not bringing on the *tapis* the restoration of the Temporal Power, and far from ignoring it, it acknowledged what the President of the Council himself had said, that important political elements (the majority of the Senators) regarded it as necessary. The statement concluded by manifesting the decided wish of the Government to be able to contribute to the independence of the Holy See and of its action, so necessary for the entire catholic world.

Political ability is put to a severe test in steer-
ing a middle course, that will avoid offence to the
susceptibilities of one side or the other. So the
diplomatic see-saw of remonstrance and satisfaction
goes on, now on one side now on the other, and
as each new incident crops up, the stereotyped
formulas of " inalterable friendship for Italy " and
" profound veneration for the Holy See," are as
surely forthcoming to restore the balance. The
equilibrium requires too delicate a poise, and is
full of danger. A slight indiscretion, or the male-
volence of a nobody, as in the case of the " Viva
il Papa! " written by one or two members of a
French pilgrimage on the register of the Pantheon,
may precipitate a catastrophe.

There is little trace of the diplomatic touch in
the frank letter of the Empress of Austria to the
Queen of Italy, published by Canon Waechtler in
his " Life of Francis Joseph," in which she expres-
ses her regret that she cannot return the visit of
the Queen at Rome. After speaking of the evils
that have befallen all persecutors of the Pope,
she continues: — " The mere thought in such circumstances of setting foot on the threshold of
the Quirinal fills me with alarm. I regret from
the bottom of my heart that I am unable to return
her visit to my Royal Sister, but the fault is not
mine, but of those who will govern the world with

a view to ephemeral and deceitful material interests." Even the Protestant Sovereigns who do sit
at the table of the King of Italy must remind him
unpleasantly of the fact that his tenure of Rome
lacks a proper sanction when they observe the
etiquette required by the Vatican in their visits to
the Pope.

Further, there is the enormous disadvantage to
Italy in the absence of Catholics from parliamentary elections and from the Chamber of Deputies
in obedience to the command of the Pope, known
as the "Non Expedit." It has been modified by
the present Pope, so that in particular cases leave
may be granted to Catholics to stand as candid-
ates for parliament, or take part in the election, but
the general law is still in force, as we were re-
minded only the other day by an inspired note in
the *Osservatore Romano*. The catholic vote is
being organized throughout the country, so that at
some future date, when the prohibition is withdrawn, it may be cast in favour of a party of order,
like the Centre Party in Germany.

The times are seemingly not yet ripe for a satisfactory solution of the Roman Question. But
while we hope and pray that the Vicar of Christ
may be soon restored to a position of independence
for the good of the Universal Church, we may not
anticipate his judgment with regard to any con-

crete scheme. It is for him alone to decide in this grave and delicate matter, and the only right attitude for loyal Catholics is to obey his instructions and support his claims. It is well expressed in the resolution of the Catholic Union of Great Britain, passed at the meeting which they held on the return of the Duke of Norfolk from Rome, where in January 1901 at the head of the British pilgrims in the Vatican (I remember well the occasion) he declared the necessity of the independence of the Pope.

The resolution ran as follows: — "On the subject of the Temporal Power the policy of the Catholic Union is very clear and simple. In this matter the Catholic Union simply follows the Vicar of Christ.

" He is the trustee on behalf of catholics generally, of that civil sovereignty which for so many ages the Roman Pontiffs have possessed. It is for him to declare, when the proper time comes, what kind of restoration to, what measure of recognition of, his legitimate rights of sovereignty, will be sufficient for that Papal independence which, in the words of the President of the Catholic Union, above referred to, 'no catholic throughout the world can afford to let go.' The position of the Catholic Union with regard to this question is most accurately described in another paragraph of His Grace's letter. 'It is not for us to say what arrangement with the Italian government would be satisfactory to the Pope. That is a question which he alone can determine. We know that the interests of the Church are safe in the hands of the Pope.'"

————

APPENDIX

Text of Law of Guarantees

Number 214 (series 2) Law on the Prerogatives of the Sovereign Pontiff and the Holy See, and on the relations of the State with the Church.

VICTOR EMMANUEL II
BY THE GRACE OF GOD AND THE WILL OF THE NATION
KING OF ITALY

The Senate and the Chamber of Deputies have approved;

We have sanctioned and promulgate what follows:

TITLE I.

Prerogatives of the Sovereign Pontiff and the Holy See.

Art. 1. The person of the Sovereign Pontiff is sacred and inviolable.

Art. 2. Any attempt against the person of the Sovereign Pontiff and provocation to commit the same shall be punished with the same penalties laid down for any attempt and for provocation to commit the same against the person of the King.

Offences and public insults commited directly against the person of the Pontiff by speeches, deeds, or the means indicated in the first article of the law on the Press, shall be punished with the penalties laid down in the 19th article of the same law.

The aforesaid breaches of the law are matter for public prosecution and belong to the competency of the Court of Assizes.

Art. 3. The Italian Government pays sovereign honours to the Supreme Pontiff in the territory of the realm; and preserves to him the preeminences of honour paid to him by Catholic Sovereigns.

The Sovereign Pontiff can retain the usual number of guards attached to his person and employed for the custody of the Palaces, without prejudice to the obligations and duties incumbent on those guards by reason of the laws in force in the realm.

Art. 4. There is preserved in favour of the Holy See the endowment of an annual revenue of 3,225,000 lire [equivalent to 129,000 pounds sterling]. With this sum, equal to that inscribed in the Roman balance sheet under this heading — *Sacred Apostolic Palaces, Sacred College, Ecclesiastical Congregations, Secretariate of State, and the Diplomatic Service abroad,* — it shall be understood that provision has been made for the support of the Sovereign Pontiff, and for the various ecclesiastical needs of the Holy See, for the maintenance ordinary and extraordinary, and the custody of the Apostolic Palaces and their dependencies; for the assignments, and payments, and pensions of the Guards, mentioned in the preceding article, and of the officials of the Papal Court, and for eventual expenses; as also for the ordinary maintenance and custody of the Museums and Library, and for the assignments, stipends and pensions of those who are therein employed.

The aforesaid endowment shall be inscribed in the Great Book of the Public Debt, in the form of perpetual and inalienable revenue in the name of the Holy See; and during the vacancy of the Holy See this payment will be continued to supply all the needs peculiar to the Roman Church in this interval.

It will be exempt from every species of tax and State, communal or provincial burden; and it cannot be diminished even in case the Italian Government shall hereafter undertake the responsibility of providing for the expenses of the Museums and Library.

Art. 5. The Sovereign Pontiff, besides the endowment established in the preceding article, continues to enjoy [*continua a godere*] the Apostolic Palaces of the Vatican and the Lateran, with all the buildings, gardens and plots connected with them, as well as

the Villa of Castel Gandolfo with all its appurtenances
and dependencies. The said palaces, villas and annexes, as also the Museums, Library and artistic and
archeological collections therein existent, are inalienable and exempt from all taxes or burdens, and
from expropriations on any ground of public utility.

Art. 6. During the vacancy of the Papal See, no
judicial or political authority shall be able, for any
reason whatsoever, to impede or limit the personal
liberty of the Cardinals.

The Government provides that the meetings of the
Conclave and of Ecumenical Councils shall not be
disturbed by any external violence.

Art. 7. No official of the Public Authority or
agent of the public force can, in the discharge of
his own office, enter the Palaces or places of ha-
bitual residence or temporary stay of the Sovereign
Pontiff, or in which is assembled a Conclave or an
Ecumenical Council, unless authorized by the Sovereign Pontiff, the Conclave, or the Ecumenical Council.

Art. 8. It is forbidden to proceed to visits, per-
quisitions, or sequestrations of papers, documents,
books, or registers in the Papal Offices or Congregations, that are invested with purely spiritual attri-
butions.

Art. 9. The Sovereign Pontiff is perfectly free to
accomplish all the functions of his Spiritual Ministry, and to post at the doors of the basilicas and

churches of Rome all the Acts of his aforesaid Ministry.

Art. 10. Ecclesiastics who by reason of their office share in Rome in the issue of the Acts of the Spiritual Ministry of the Holy See, are not liable, on account of these, to any molestation, investigation, or calling to account on the part of the Public Authority.

Every foreign subject invested with an ecclesiastical office in Rome enjoys the personal guarantees belonging to Italian subjects in virtue of the Laws of the Realm.

Art. 11. The Envoys of Foreign Governments to His Holiness enjoy in the Kingdom all the prerogatives and immunities which belong to Diplomatic Agents according to International Law.

To offences against them are extended the penal sanctions for offences against the Envoys of Foreign Powers to the Italian Government.

To the Envoys of His Holiness to Foreign Governments are assured, in the territory of the Kingdom, the customary prerogatives and immunities, according to the same Law, in going to and returning from the place of their mission.

Art. 12. The Sovereign Pontiff corresponds freely with the Episcopate and with the whole Catholic world, without any interference of the Italian Government.

9

For this purpose he can establish in the Vatican or in any other residence of his, post and telegraph offices, served by *employés* of his own choice.

The Papal post office can send its correspondence in a closed packet directly to the postal offices of exchange of Foreign Administrations, or commit the same to the Italian offices.

In both cases the forwarding of despatches and correspondence bearing the stamp of the Papal office shall be exempt from all tax and expense in Italian territory.

Couriers sent in the name of the Sovereign Pontiff are regarded in the Kingdom as on a level with the ministerial couriers of Foreign Governments.

The Papal telegraph office shall be united with the telegraphic system of the Kingdom at the expense of the State.

Telegrams despatched from the said office with the authentic qualification of *Papal,* shall be received and sent on with the prerogatives established for State telegrams, and with exemption from all tax in the Kingdom.

Telegrams of the Supreme Pontiff, or those signed by his order, which, bearing the stamp of the Holy See, may he presented at any telegraph office in the Kingdom, shall enjoy the same advantages.

Telegrams addressed to the Sovereign Pontiff shall be exempt from the payments to be exacted from the receiver.

Art. 13. In the City of Rome, and in the Suburbicarian Sees, the Seminaries, Academies, Colleges, and other Catholic Institutes founded for the education and culture of ecclesiastics, shall continue to depend solely on the Holy See, without any interference of the Educational Authorities of the Realm.

TITLE II.

Relations of the State with the Church.

. . . .

We order that the present, stamped with the seal of the State, shall be inserted in the *Official Collection* of the Laws and Decrees of the Kingdom of Italy, commanding everybody whom it may concern to observe it and cause it to be observed as a law of the State.

Given in Turin, 13 May, 1871.

VICTOR EMMANUEL.

G. LANZA — VISCONTI-VENOSTA — G. DE FALCO — Q. SELLA — C. CORRENTI — E. RICOTTI — C. ACTON — S. CASTAGNOLA — G. GADDA.

9 *

INDEX

CHAPTER I.

CHAPTER II.

Chapter VI.

The unique character of the Papal Temporal Power.

Chapter VII.

Radical defects in the Law of Guarantees

Negotiations fail — Italy acting in her own name — The
only guarantee the word of the Pope's despoilers — The
Law internal and subject to change — A narrow interpretation of its internal character — Internal laws have
sometimes an international scope — Important decision of
the Council of State recognizing international scope of the
Law of Guarantees — The Law dependent upon a parliamentary majority — Movement for its abolition — The
great obstacle — Sig. Bonghi's view — The Law more
necessary to Italy than to the Pope.

Chapter VIII.

Further defects of the Law of Guarantees . . p. 75

The instability of the Law of Guarantees not a subject of
complaint with the Pope — The nature of the independence offered to the Pope — No subjects, no territory —
The Pope a tenant-at-will of the King of Italy — The
Republic of San Marino and United Italy — The Roman
Plebiscite a farce — A Plebiscite not legitimate ground
for a change of dynasty — Alsace and Lorraine, Heligoland, the Federal District of Columbia — The miserable
allowance set apart for the Holy See — Proposed method
of payment most offensive to the Holy See.

Chapter IX.

Diplomatic Relations and Pontifical Acts under the Law . . . . p. 83

Text of the Law on Diplomatic Relations with the Holy See
— Permanent relations between the Holy See and Foreign
Powers — Occasional missions — These relations not due
to a concession of the Law — Italy cannot abolish them,

nor control them in time of peace — The Pope's freedom
of communication curtailed in time of war — Supreme
interests of the Church dependent on the good-will of
Italy — Publication of Papal Acts allowed to ecclesiastics,
their approval liable to punishment — General review of
the Law — Its sovereignty a mockery.

Chapter XII.